Disney LEARNING

Disney LEARNING

This workbook belongs to:

____

Published by Nelson Education Ltd.

ISBN-13: 978-0-17-689217-3
ISBN-10: 0-17-689217-6

Printed and bound in Canada
1 2 3 4 22 21 20 19

For more information contact Nelson Education Ltd.,
1120 Birchmount Road, Toronto, Ontario M1K 5G4.
Or you can visit our website at nelson.com.

Credits: 100: (Coin images) © 2017 Royal Canadian Mint. All rights reserved. 105: Shapiro Svetlana/Shutterstock.com. 107: (soccer and basketball) Yuliyan Velchev/Shutterstock.com; (bowling ball) BlueRingMedia/Shutterstock.com. 132: (Coin images) © 2017 Royal Canadian Mint. All rights reserved. 133: (Coin images) © 2017 Royal Canadian Mint. All rights reserved. 150: (top to bottom) Nelson Education Ltd; Mega Pixel/Shutterstock.com; Victorija Reuta/Shutterstock .com. 153: Coffeemill/Shutterstock.com; Monkey Business Images/Shutterstock.com. 154: (left to right) Konrad Mostert/Shutterstock.com; AlexussK/ Shutterstock.com; Anna Kucherova/Shutterstock.com; Ipbombaert/Shutterstock.com; Hurst Photo; ericlefrancais/Shutterstock.com; rilence/Shutterstock.com; Ivan Volozhanin/Shutterstock.com; Lev Kropotov/Shutterstock.com. 155: (top to bottom) Ivan Volozhanin/Shutterstock.com; Danny Smythe/Shutterstock.com; vvoe/Shutterstock.com; Kovalchuk Oleksandr/Shutterstock.com. 156: (left to right) Venus Angel/Shutterstock.com; Madien/Shutterstock/com; suns07butterfly/ Shutterstock.com; Utekhina Anna/Shutterstock.com. 157: Photology 1971/Shutterstock.com. 163: Dmitry Zimin/Shutterstock.com. 162: (top to bottom) Miyuki Satake/Shutterstock.com; Miyuki Satake/Shutterstock.com; Miyuki Satake/Shutterstock.com. 167: (top to bottom) Dmitry Zimin/Shutterstock.com; Dmitry Zimin/Shutterstock.com. 174: Nelson Education Ltd. 175: Nelson Education Ltd. 176: (bottom) Nelson Education Ltd.

Contents

Ready to Read and Write

Letter Recognition 2
Word Knowledge.................................. 36
Comprehension 48
Writing 64

Ready for Math

Number Sense 78
Patterns 86
Addition and Subtraction.................. 92
Multiplication and Division.............. 108
Measurement..................................... 118
Geometry... 130
Collecting and Using Data............. 138

What's Next? 142
Glossary 146
Answers 150

A Magical Alphabet

Elsa and Anna are sisters.

Elsa has a magical power.

She can freeze things and create snow and ice with her hands!

Fill in the missing capital letters below.

A B C D ___E___ F G H I ___J___ K L ___m___

N ___o___ P Q ___R___ S T U ___V___ W X Y Z

Fill in the missing lowercase letters below.

a ____ c d e ____ g h i ____ k l ____

n o p ____ r s t ____ v w ____ y z

Learn Together

Play a game with your child: say the alphabet, pausing randomly so your child can name a word beginning with the last letter you listed.

Ordering the Letters

Does Elsa have powers?

Did you notice that the words in the above sentence are in alphabetical order?

Alphabetical order is when the letters of the alphabet are in the correct sequence.

A B C D E F G H I J K L M N O
P Q R S T U V W X Y Z

Put these words in alphabetical order to make a sentence.

powers magical Elsa has.

____.

Unlock the order of these letters.

Put each group of letters in alphabetical order.

The first one has been done for you.

B D A

ABD

A K T

AKt

d h f o

dfho

z d r f

dfrz

U x j q

jqux

h Y O S

hosY

I r q B

Blqr

W j D k

DjKW

Learn Together Your child may still need some help putting letters in alphabetical order. With your child, list characters from *Frozen*. Help your child arrange the names in **alphabetical order**.

Alphabet Exploration

Anna can explore now!

Did you notice that the words in the above sentence are in alphabetical order?

Put each set of words in alphabetical order.

waterfront boat people

____

kingdom castle Arendelle

____

shop dress horse

____

Hans charming prince

snow Elsa queen

gates love Anna

Learn Together

Help your child read the words and sort them into alphabetical order. Use some of these words to tell a story about the Frozen characters.

Lets Get Ready!

R J B H S W L A O

Elsa needs to get ready for her coronation.
Put these words in alphabetical order.

summer coronation room

____

gloves scepter orb

____

hall dance magic

____

Put these words in alphabetical order to create sentences.

queen Elsa is

____.

purple Elsa likes

____.

Anna dance can sing or

____.

playing Anna enjoys

____.

Learn Together

Challenge your child to create a sentence with all the words in alphabetical order. How many words can they use and still have all of them in alphabetical order? (A two-word sentence is easier than three, three easier than four, and so on.)

Missing Letters

Can you figure out which letter is missing?

Use each purple letter only once.

_____ights	_____ere	h l r t
_____oyal	_____own	

Read each word out loud.

Listen to the sound of the first letter.

Add the missing letters.

h l r t

It's ___ime for Elsa's coronation.

Elsa will become queen ___ere in the main ___all.

Many people wait in ___ine to see ___oyalty.

Read each sentence out loud.

Listen to the letter sounds.

Learn Together

Help your child sound out the words and use **context** to complete the sentences. Emphasize the consonant sounds as you say each word.

More Missing Letters

Can you figure out which letter is missing?

______ister　　______ance

______allroom　　______alk

d　　s　　b　　w

Read each word out loud.

Listen to the sound of the first letter.

Add the missing letters.

d s b w

Anna and Hans spend time at the ___all

Hans asks Anna if she ___ould like to ___ance.

They laugh and ___alk together.

It is love at first ___ight.

Hans asks Anna if she ___ill marry him.

Anna is happy. She ___ays yes!

Read each sentence out loud.

Listen to the letter sounds.

Learn Together

Help your child sound out the words and use **context** to complete the sentences. Emphasize the consonant sounds as you say each word.

Magical Frozen Letters

Some letters are frozen.

Can you figure out which letter is missing?

Use each purple letter only once.

______arty	______ight	n f
______amily	______agic	m p

Read each word out loud.

Listen to the sound of the first letter.

Add the missing letters. n m f p

Anna and Hans ask Elsa to bless their ___arriage.

Elsa does ___ot give her ___ermission.

Elsa is ___irm. Anna ___eels upset.

Anna accidentally ___ulls off Elsa's glove.

Elsa flees the castle as her ___agic spills out.

Read each sentence out loud.

Listen to the letter sounds.

Learn Together

Help your child sound out the words and use **context** to complete the sentences. Emphasize the consonant sounds as you say each word.

A Chilly End

The townspeople know about Elsa's powers.

Add the missing letter to the end of each word.
Use each purple letter only once.

ma______ loo______

alway______ fro______

p s m k

Listen to the sound of the last letter.

Add the missing letter to
the end of each word.

p s m k

The kingdo___ is in an uproar as ice spread___.

Anna finally understand___ why Elsa keep___ to herself.

Anna set___ out to find Elsa.

She wants to bring Elsa bac___ to thaw out the kingdo___.

Anna leaves to go u___ the mountain.

Read each sentence out loud.

Listen to the letter sounds.

Learn Together

Help your child try each of the four letters until they find the right one. Note that more than one letter will work on page 16 (loop, loom, look). For each sentence, they can use context to figure out the right letter.

How Will It All End?

Elsa feels free.

Elsa lets all her powers loose!

You also have a power.

Add the missing letter to the end of each word.

d **t** **n** **l**

ligh______ quee______

coo______ win______

Read each word out loud.

Listen to the sound of the last letter.

Use one of the words to write a sentence about Elsa.

____

Add the missing letter to the end of each word.
Hint: If two letters are missing in a word, it is the same letter.

d n t l

Elsa climbs high up the mountai___.

Elsa uses her powers to buil___ a___ amazing ice palace.

She feels like the perso___ she is mean___ to be!

She knows it wi___ ___ be lonely in her ice palace.

A___ long las___, Elsa knows she wi___ ___ be free!

Read each sentence out loud.

Listen to the letter sounds.

Learn Together

Discuss how the word *will* uses double consonants at the end. Can your child think of other words with double consonants (off, pull, boss)? With your child, list rhyming words for some of the words on this page (bill, till, mill; fast, past, cast). Emphasize the ending sound as you read the list over.

Vowel Journey

Anna goes to the trading post.
Will she buy a **hat**?

The letter **a** can make a short vowel sound, as in **hat**.

The letter **a** can also make a long vowel sound, as in **trade**.
Long vowels sound like their letter names.

Say each word out loud.
Listen for the vowel sound.

Circle the words that have a short vowel **a** sound.

bat map rake bag grab

vase sash race

Underline the words that have a long vowel **a** sound.

apple mad cake mat way

mane game drain

Anna **meets** Kristoff and **Sven** at the trading post.

The letter **e** can make a short vowel sound, as in **Sven**. The letter **e** can also make a long vowel sound, as in **meet**

Circle the words that have a short vowel **e** sound.

bed   bee   jet   hen   get

bead   feet   red

Underline the that have with a long vowel **e** sound.

fed   leaf   met   seal   meal

set   we   test

Learn Together

With your child, identify the vowel pattern or rule in some of the words above (When two vowels appear together in a word, the first vowel is usually long and the second is silent, as in *maid* and *beat*.).

Bit or Bite

The letter **i** can make a short vowel sound, as in **mitt**.

The letter **i** can also make a long vowel sound, as in **ice**.

Say each word out loud.
Listen for the vowel sound.

Circle the words that have a short vowel **i** sound.

gift bit fine time

side if king

Underline the words that have a long vowel **i** sound.

I pin vine fire fish

bite it line

The letter **o** can make a short vowel sound, as in **hot**.

The letter **o** can also make a long vowel sound, as in **cold**.

Circle the words that have a short vowel **o** sound.

mop rope box rob robe

odd pot log

Underline the words that have a long vowel **o** sound.

open road lock ocean doll

sock note pod

Learn Together

With your child, look for patterns in these words (A silent **e** at the end of a word—*robe*—makes the vowel in the middle long. Most three-letter words with a consonant, vowel, consonant have a short vowel sound—*rob*.).

Cut to the Cute

The new friends travel together.

The letter **u** can make a short vowel sound, as in **uphill**.
The letter **u** can also make a long vowel sound, as in **use**.

Say each word out loud.
Listen for the vowel sound.

Circle the words that have a short vowel **u** sound.

cut rescue hut mug plum

truck sun music

Underline the words that have a long vowel **u** sound.

duck cube use cute

unite bug unicorn

The letter y can sometimes act as a vowel.

What letter sound does the y make in **funny**? ______

What letter sound does the y make in **fry**? ______

Say each of these words out loud.

Write the vowel sound you hear.

The first one has been done for you.

cry __i__	shy ______	fly ______
jelly ______	silly ______	baby ______

The letter y can sometimes work with a vowel to make a long vowel sound.

Say these words out loud: **bay** **they** **hay** **pay**

Learn Together

Discuss the vowel sounds. In the **ay** words, the **y** acts to make the **a** long. In *they,* the **y** does not make a long **e** sound. As your child's reading skills develop, they will notice many other exceptions to general rules.

R-Controlled Vowels

Wolves come out in the **dark**.

Sometimes, other letters can make vowels sound different.

For example, in the word **charge**, **a** sounds different when followed by **r**.

The **a** in charge does not sound long or short.

The **r** changes the sound of the vowel.

Add the missing vowels.

m___rbles b___rd n___rse f___rk

c___r tig___r b___rn sk___rt

doct___r t___rkey w___rd

Say each word out loud.
Listen to the vowel sound.

The letter **w** can also change the sound of a vowel.

Read these sentences out loud.

We **saw** you through the **window**.

The **jaw** **yawns**.

Will you **plow** with the **cow**?

Take a **bow**, **now**.

Listen to the vowel sound in the **purple** words.

Did you notice that you don't pronounce the **w** on its own?

The vowel plus **w** makes one sound.

Learn Together

Help your child figure out the missing letters. In some cases, more than one vowel will work (burn, barn; ward, word). As you read together, look for words that follow similar patterns.

Freezing Words

The wolves chase the friends!

Sometimes when two consonants work together in a word you hear both letter sounds.

For example, you can hear both the **f** and the **r** in **frozen**.

Choose one pair of consonants to make a word.

br tr sl ______ick	cl fr bl ______og
fr br ch ______eeze	fl bl cl ______ock
cl br sl ______ing	dr cr st ______eam

Sven pulls a sled. What two consonants work together in **sled**? ________

Choose one pair of consonants to make a word.

fr **tr** **cl** **bl** **sp** **sl**

________ee

________ock

________iend

________ow

________ide

________in

Learn Together

Your child can make a variety of words with each consonant pair and **word ending**. See **consonant blends** in the glossary for more on how consonants work together at the beginning and end of words.

Sticking Together to the End

Two or more consonants can also work together at the end of a word.

Olaf is Anna's **friend**.

Listen to the sounds the letters **nd** make.

Choose one pair of consonants to make a word.

lp nt lt he_____	st pt ct te_____
nt nd mp ba_____	pt nt mp la_____
st lp rd bi_____	lf nt rd elepha_____

Choose one pair of consonants to make a word.
More than one pair of consonants may work.

st ck rd st mp nd

sti__________

be__________

du__________

grou__________

wo__________

la __________

be __________

Learn Together

Review more consonant blends (**-sk**, **-sp**, **-ld**, **-rk**). With your child, create flash cards with a word ending on one side and words in that **word family** on the other side.

When Words Work

The friends work together to find Elsa.

Sometimes **when** two consonants work together in a word you hear only one sound.

For example, the **t** and **h** in **the** and the **w** and **h** in **when**.

Choose one pair of consonants to make a word.

sh th ch ______en	th wh ch ______orn	ch th wr ______eat
sh ch th ______eet	wh sh th ______ut	sh wh th ______ark
wh wr th ______ale	sh ch wr ______ite	sh ch wr ______eese

Choose one pair of consonants to make a word.

ch **sh** **th** **wh** **wr**

______________________ ______________________

______________________ ______________________

____

Learn Together

Your child can make a variety of words with **digraphs** such as these. List other words in the **wr** or **wh** word family (write, written, wrote; whale, what, which).

Unfreeze the Silent Letters

Kristoff rushes to help Anna.

Elsa does not want to **talk**.

Did you know that letters can be silent, too?

These letters are called **silent consonants**.

The letters **b**, **g**, **h**, **k**, **l**, **t**, and **w** are sometimes silent.

Do you know any words with silent letters?

Say each of these words out loud.

Underline the silent letters.

castle listen lamb

two comb ghost talk hour

honest light knife sign

Say each of these words out loud.

Underline the silent letters.

walk sight wheel knee sword

when rhyme climb write knight

gnome fight wrap know

Learn Together Create word family lists for the **silent letters**. For example, record all the words your child knows that include the letters **gh** or **kn**.

Do You Want to Build a Word?

Marshmallow the **snowman** chases the friends away from the palace.

A **compound word** is made using two smaller words.

Draw a / between the two smaller words in the word below.

snowman

Draw a / between the two smaller words in each word below.

The first one has been done for you.

can/not	pancake	rainbow	bathtub
snowball	hairbrush	grasshopper	without
cupcake	backpack	sunshine	earring

Match a word on the left to a word on the right to make a compound word.

hall	flake
fire	way
snow	fast
bed	place
break	room

Circle the compound words below.

handbag	glasses	birthday	jackpot
daydream	flattery	winter	snowflake

Learn Together

Help your child find the little words inside bigger words when reading books together. These little words can often give clues to the meaning of the **compound word**.

Don't Look Down!

A **contraction** is a word that is made by joining two words.

An **apostrophe** takes the place of any missing letters.

Match each contraction below with the two words that have been joined.

we're	I am
don't	you are
you're	he is
he's	do not
I'm	we are

Fill in the missing contraction to complete each sentence.

He's

don't

They're

The friends run away from Marshmallow.

___ ___ ' ___ upset.

___ ___ ___ ___' ___ ___ scared of Marshmallow.

The friends run until they reach a cliff.

They ___ ___ ___' ___ wait to jump.

Use one of the contractions to write a sentence about Marshmallow.

____

Learn Together

With your child, create flash cards with a **contraction** on one side and the two words that form that contraction on the other. Use the cards to play matching games.

Before the Snowstorm

Prefixes are added to the start of a root word. Together, they make a new word with a different meaning.

pre + made = premade

un + happy = unhappy

re + write = rewrite

pre + view = preview

un + done = undone

re + play = replay

Think about the words above. Match up each prefix below with its meaning.

un	**before**
pre	**again**
re	**not**

Fill in the missing prefix to complete each sentence below.

You may use each prefix more than once.

Elsa is ___ ___happy because she can't ___ ___freeze Arendelle.

She ___ ___plays the party in her head.

___ ___fortunately, Elsa will soon have more problems.

Will Elsa be able to ___ ___do what she has done?

un

re

Add a prefix to a word to make a new word.

_______________ + _______________ = _______________

Learn Together

Help your child choose a **prefix** to complete each sentence. they need more than one prefix for some sentences. Help your child choose prefixes as they complete the sentences above.

More and Most

The friends ask the trolls for help.

Suffixes are added to the end of a word to make a new word. For example, Baby Trolls are **big**, but Grand Pabble is **bigger**. Who is the **biggest**?

Add the root word to its suffix.

soft + er = ______________________

soft + est = ______________________

soft + ness = ______________________

Try adding **-er**, **-est**, and **-ness** to each of the following words.

sweet ____________ ________________ __________________

kind ____________ ________________ __________________

bright ____________ ________________ __________________

Learn Together

With your child, read the words on the page. Help them work out the meaning of each word with its **suffix**. Encourage them to use the words in sentences.

Person, Place, and Thing

A **noun** is a word for a person, a place, or a thing.

Read the nouns out loud.

person:	Anna	sister	friend	everyone
place:	Arendelle	city	castle	house
thing:	snowball	carrot	chocolate	sled

In the sentences below, the nouns have been underlined:

<u>Elsa's</u> <u>magic</u> has frozen <u>Anna's</u> <u>heart</u>.

<u>Kristoff</u>, <u>Sven</u>, and <u>Olaf</u> take <u>Anna</u> back to <u>Arendelle</u>.

<u>Anna</u> needs to get to <u>Hans</u>.

Only an <u>act</u> of true <u>love</u> can thaw <u>Anna's</u> frozen <u>heart</u>!

Underline the nouns in each sentence.

Anna finds Hans in the library .

"If only someone loved you Anna," Hans says with a sneer. Hans has been lying to Anna!

Learn Together

With your child, list five people, five places, and five things. Help your child make silly sentences using the items on the list (*Dad*, *kitchen*, and *spoon* can become "Dad is dancing with a spoon in the kitchen.").

Action!

A **verb** is an action word.

A verb often follows a noun.

The verb is the "doing" word.

Underline the verbs below.

gallop candle race grab laugh shiver

spin yell ocean eat carrot palace

Pick an action word.

Draw a picture of Olaf doing that action.

When you add a verb to a sentence, how the verb is spelled depends on the noun it appears with. **We run** fast, but **she runs** faster.

Underline the verbs below. Think about how the verb is spelled.

Hans douses the fire.

Hans has tricked Anna.

"No, stop," Anna says as she reaches forward.

"Nothing can stop me now." Hans says as he locks the door.

Anna is trapped!

Learn Together

Your child is probably already following the rules for **verbs** and nouns naturally as they speak. Practise writing sentences together using a noun and verb that agree.

Storm Over Arendelle

Clues in the text and picture can help you **make predictions.**

Look at the picture. Predict what the story on page 49 is about. ______________________________

______________________________.

Sven stops Kristoff.

Sven knows that Kristoff is in love with Anna.

A large storm starts to form above Arendelle!

Sven urges Kristoff to go back to Arendelle to save Anna before it is too late.

I'm sure that ______________________________

will go back to Arendelle to save Anna because __________

____

____.

Learn Together

Help your child read this story, look for clues, and **make predictions**. When reading other stories, encourage your child to look for clues. Before you turn a page, ask your child what they think will happen next.

That Reminds Me . . .

Reading stories can remind us of our own lives.

Anna gives up all hope. Suddenly, Olaf arrives and helps Anna to start a fire.

Anna tells Olaf about Hans.

Olaf looks out the window and sees Kristoff and Sven heading towards the castle.

Olaf and Anna both realize that Kristoff is the one true love that can save her.

"I have to get to Kristoff," Anna says to Olaf.

Underline the words in the story that remind you of something.

Explain any connections you made.

____

____.

Learn Together

Help your child read this story. Encourage them to find different ways that a story connects to their own life. Model **making connections** ("This story reminds me of a time when I . . ."). Ask them questions ("Do you remember when you . . . ?").

What, Where, and Who

Story elements include the plot, setting, and characters.

The **plot** is what happens—the problem or events in the story.

The **setting** is where the story happens.

The **characters** are who the story is about.

Olaf helps Anna to the frozen fjord.

Only an act of true love can thaw a frozen heart.

Anna believes only Kristoff can save her.

Suddenly, Anna spots Hans about to attack Elsa!

Anna runs to Elsa. She has to help her sister.

Circle the characters in this story.

Underline the setting.

Number the events in the story.

Learn Together

Help your child read this story and identify its elements. With your child, generate ideas for another story. On a piece of paper, draw three boxes. In each box, your child can record ideas for the **story elements**: characters, setting, and plot.

Describe It!

An **adjective** is a word that describes a noun.

Elsa is **sad**. The word **sad** describes **Elsa**.

Add one of these adjectives to a sentence below.

big **scared** **blue**

Elsa has ___ ___ ___ ___ eyes.

Elsa is feeling ___ ___ ___ ___ ___ ___.

Elsa has a ___ ___ ___ problem.

Write a sentence to describe yourself.

Use an adjective.

____

An **adverb** is a word that describes a verb.

It tells when, where, how, or what.

These are adverbs:

now, **loudly**, **under**, **inside**, **carefully**

Elsa cries **sadly**.

The word **sadly** describes **how** Elsa is crying.

Add each of these adverbs to a sentence below.

softly **deeply** **always** **outside**

Elsa sits on the ice ___ ___ ___ ___ ___ ___ ___.

Elsa cares ___ ___ ___ ___ ___ ___ for her sister.

She whispers ___ ___ ___ ___ ___ ___.

Elsa ___ ___ ___ ___ ___ ___ thinks about her sister.

Learn Together

Ask your child to describe household items using adjectives. Encourage them to consider colour, shapes, smells, and textures. Give your child prompts to complete with adverbs ("The turtle moved ______." "The siren blared ____.").

Picture It!

As you read, use the words in the text to make **pictures** in your mind.

Anna runs to Elsa!

With her remaining strength, Anna throws herself in front of Elsa.

Anna reaches out to block Han's sharp sword.

Suddenly, Anna turns to solid ice.

Han's sword shatters making a loud CLANK.

Underline the words that help you form a picture of the scene in your mind.

Describe what you see. ____

____

____.

Learn Together

Cover up the image on page 56 as you read the description on this page so that your child has the opportunity to visualize the scene.

Look for the Clues

When you read, you put together the clues the author gives you. You "read between the lines" or **make inferences** to understand the text.

Elsa wraps her arms around her frozen sister.

Elsa begins to cry. Then something amazing happens. Suddenly, Anna begins to thaw!

"You sacrificed yourself for me?" Elsa asks.

"Of course, I love you," Anna replies.

An act of true love thaws Anna's heart.

Elsa smiles at her sister.

Elsa is happy that Anna is safe.

How do you think Elsa is feeling?

____

____

Learn Together

Read the story to your child and model **making inferences** ("I think Elsa is happy to have her sister back. She was scared to have lost Anna.").

I Think . . . Because . . .

When you **draw conclusions**, you are forming an opinion or making a decision about what you have just read.
Good conclusions are based on facts in the text.

Hans is surprised to see that Anna is alive.

"But Elsa froze your heart," Hans says.

"The only frozen heart around here is yours." Anna declares.

Before Hans can respond Anna sends him flying with just one punch!

"That's what you get for trying to hurt my sister!" Anna states.

Do you agree with Anna's actions? Why?

____

____

Learn Together

Talk about this story and the questions. Help your child practise **drawing conclusions** by talking about the characters and events in other stories ("Why did the character do that? Do you think they were right? What would you have done?").

Fact or Opinion?

When you read nonfiction, **most** of the text will be **facts**.

Facts are what really happened or information that is true.

Sometimes, authors include **opinions**.

Opinions are what someone believes or thinks.

Opinions can also express a feeling.

This is a fact: Most snowmen have two eyes.

This is an opinion: I think all snowmen should be tall.

Write **F** beside each fact and **O** beside each opinion.

______ I think Olaf is the best snowman.

______ Snowmen are made from snow.

______ Winter is better than summer.

______ Ice is cold.

______ I don't like sledding.

______ Elsa and Anna are sisters.

Learn Together

Read this text to your child. With your child, write a few sentences about a topic they like (hockey, animals, music). Underline the **facts**. Write **O** beside any **opinions**. Encourage your child to support their opinions.

Extra Information

Labels give you extra information.

They help you understand pictures better.

Fill in the missing labels. The first label is done for you.

Captions are sentences that tell you what is happening in a picture.

They can give you more information about the picture.

Write a caption for each picture.

____

Learn Together

Your child's labels do not have to be "correct," especially if they are not familiar with this story. Check that they are accurately describing what is in the image. Provide them with family photos that they can write labels and captions for.

Writing a Story

There are many kinds of **stories**.

There are funny stories and scary stories.

All stories have characters, a setting, and a plot.

What story does this picture tell?

Think about a story you want to tell.

Write your story.

Learn Together

Your child might want to draw illustrations for their story before they write. Beforehand, discuss their favourite kinds of stories (scary, funny, adventure, animal, etc.). Why do they like these stories? Who are the characters? What happens?

So True!

Facts are things that are true.

You can prove facts.

For example, Anna and Elsa live in Arendelle.

Anna and Elsa lose their parents at a young age.

Kristoff is an ice harvester.

Sven is Kristoff's best friend.

Write three facts about Anna, Elsa, or Kristoff.

1. ______________________________

____

____

2. ______________________________

____

____

3. ______________________________

____

____

Learn Together

Your child can use the picture to help them write facts. Or help your child research a character. List point-form facts that your child can use to help them write complete sentences.

Writing Sentences

Sentences end in different types of **punctuation**.

Kristoff is taking Anna to meet the trolls.

What is following Kristoff and Anna?

A sentence that ends with a period is telling you something.

A sentence that ends with a question mark is asking a question.

Write a sentence about Anna and Elsa that ends with a period or question mark. ______________________

____

Elsa is running away!

Elsa, wait please!

A sentence that ends with an exclamation mark can show excitement or surprise.

An exclamation mark at the end of a sentence can also be a command.

Write a sentence about Anna and Elsa that ends with an exclamation mark. ______________________________

____

Learn Together With your child, take turns writing sentences about yourselves that end with different punctuation marks. Remind them to use a capital letter at the beginning of each sentence.

A Small Pause

Commas are used to show pauses in sentences.

This is a comma: ,

With summer restored, the visiting ships sailed away

Arendelle returned to normal, but now the castle gates were open for good!

Commas can also show a list of items.

Olaf is joyful, curious, and playful.

Add the missing commas to the sentences below.

I like to eat cereal oranges and oatmeal.

____

After breakfast I get ready for school.

____

If it is cold you should wear a hat.

____

I like skiing skating and sledding.

____

Learn Together

Help your child write sentences, with commas, about their favourite character. With your child, review sentences they have written previously, looking for opportunities to include commas or other punctuation they are learning about.

Belonging and More

An **apostrophe** can be used to show that something belongs to someone.

This is an apostrophe: ’

Anna is Elsa’s sister.

Anna’s friends are Kristoff, Olaf, and Sven.

Add an apostrophe to each sentence.

Anna s parents are lost at sea.

Olaf s nose is a carrot.

A **contraction** is two words put together.

The missing letters are replaced by an apostrophe.

For example, **is not** becomes **isn't**.

Make contractions with the words below, adding an apostrophe.

they have ______________ he is ______________

you are ______________ should not ______________

she is ______________ let us ______________

would not ______________ we are ______________

should not ______________ I have ______________

Learn Together

Help your child list more contractions. Look for contractions in a story. Have your child point them out and say the two words that make the contraction.

Say It

Quotation marks show that someone is speaking. These are quotation marks: “ ”

These marks are often used with the words **said** or **asked**.

“This guy is a crook!” says Kristoff.

“Are you ready to go up the mountain?” Anna asks Kristoff.

Look at the picture on the right. Write what Kristoff’s reply might be. Use quotation marks.

Write a story about a time you met someone new.

What did you say to each other?

Use quotation marks.

Learn Together

Look at family photos with your child. Imagine the people in the photos are having conversations. Write down what they're saying using quotation marks.

Speed Counts

How fast can Olaf go?

Count **forward** using these number lines.

Print the missing numbers.

10 20 30 60 80

65 75 80 95

186 188 190 194 198

25 50 100 125 175

Print the missing numbers on the 100-chart.

100	101	102		104	105	106		108	109
110	111	112		114	115	116	117	118	119
120		122	123	124	125	126	127	128	129
	131	132	133	134	135	136	137	138	139
140	141	142	143	144	145	146	147	148	149
150	151	152	153		155	156	157	158	159
160	161	162	163	164	165	166		168	169
170	171	172	173	174	175	176	177	178	
180	181	182	183	184	185		187	188	189
190	191	192	193	194	195	196	197	198	

Learn Together

Find opportunities to practise **skip counting** to 200, either by twos, fives, or tens. You might play hide-and-seek together, bounce a ball, or jump rope.

Story Time Frames

How many candles is King Agnarr holding? ________

Draw 22 candles.

Circle groups of 10 candles.

There are ________ groups of 10 candles.

There are ________ candles left.

Show your candles in these 10-frames.

Show 22 another way.

Learn Together

Your child can use counters (buttons, beads) to fill the **10-frames** with different amounts (25, 17, 29). Every time they create a new arrangement, ask them to count the groups of 10 and then say the total.

The Greatest

Anna and Elsa are listening to great stories about the Enchanted Forest.

In each box, which number is **greater**?

Circle the greater number.

29 26	18 11	24 30	21 19
20 16	28 15	41 46	16 12
44 47	32 25	23 14	40 38

Mark each pair of numbers on the number line.

Circle the number that is **greater**.

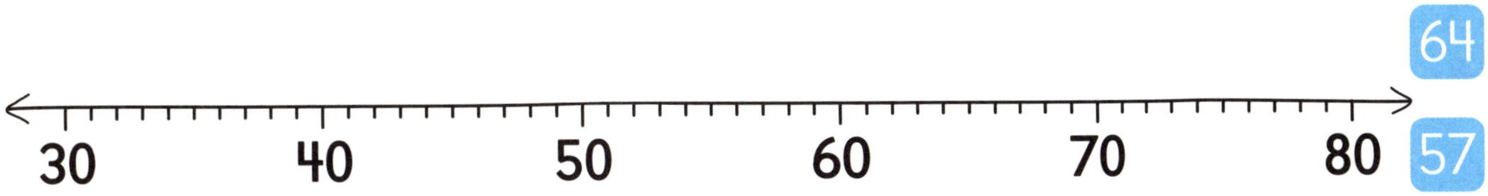

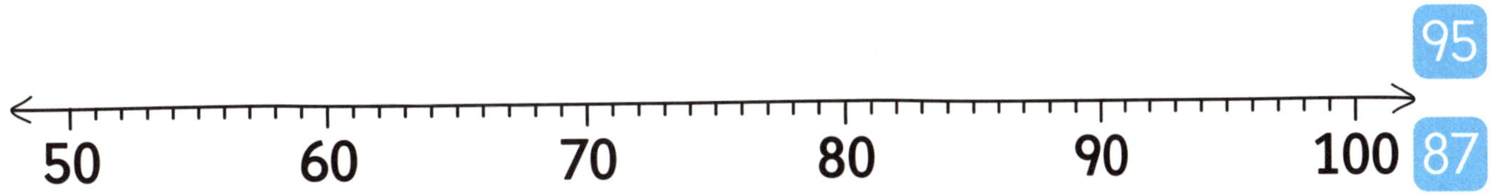

Learn Together

Use 10-frames or number lines to help your child put number sets in order from least to greatest (87, 65, 70; 82, 98, 86; 68, 83, 100). As they master sets of three, introduce a fourth number to each set.

Just a Fraction

The wall of mist separates the Enchanted Forest from the rest of the land.

A part of a whole is called a **fraction**.

When there are **2** equal parts, we call each part a **half**.

One half can be shown as $\frac{1}{2}$.

Colour **half** of each shape below.
The first one has been done for you.

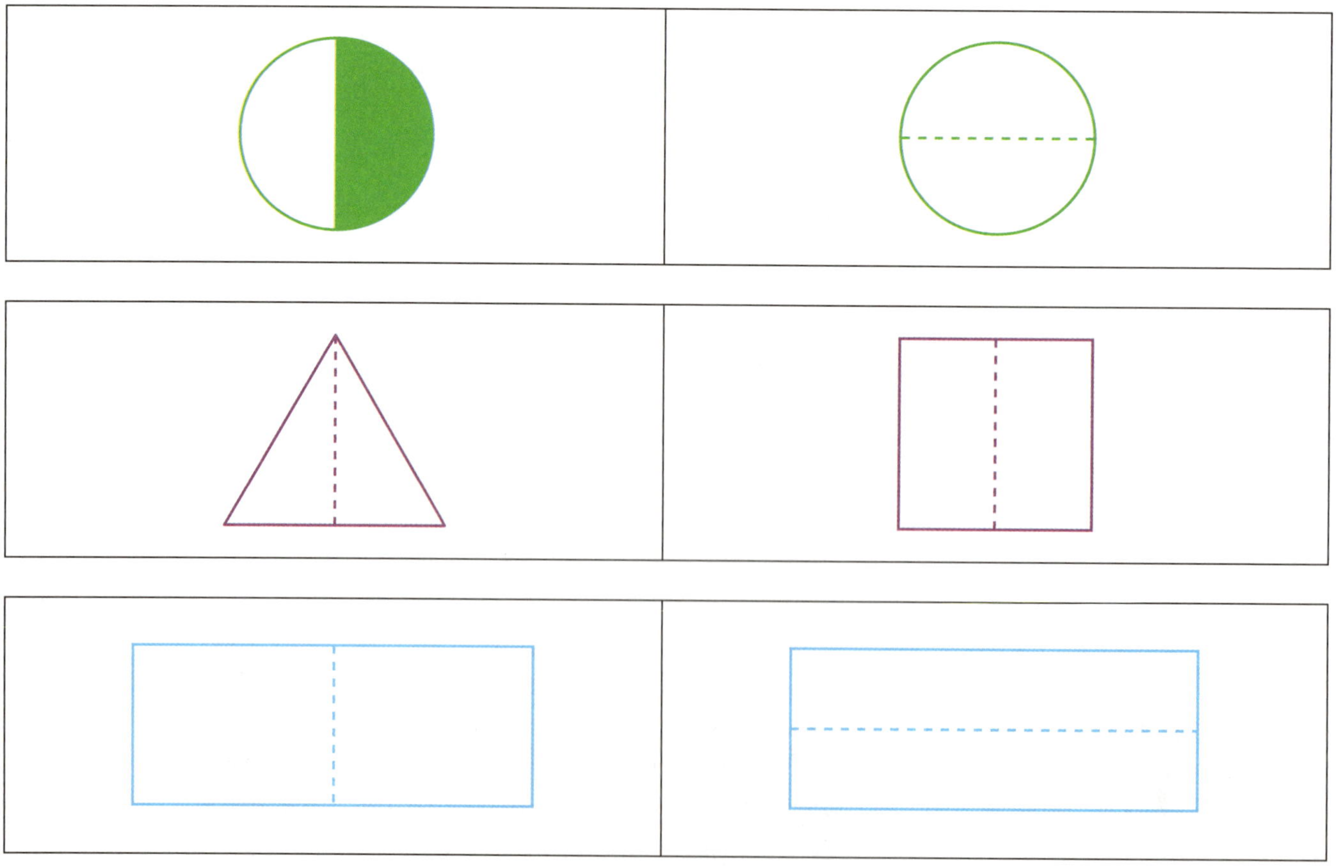

When there are 4 equal parts,
we call each part
a **fourth** or a **quarter**.

One quarter can be shown as $\frac{1}{4}$.

Colour one **fourth** of each shape below.

The first one has been done for you.

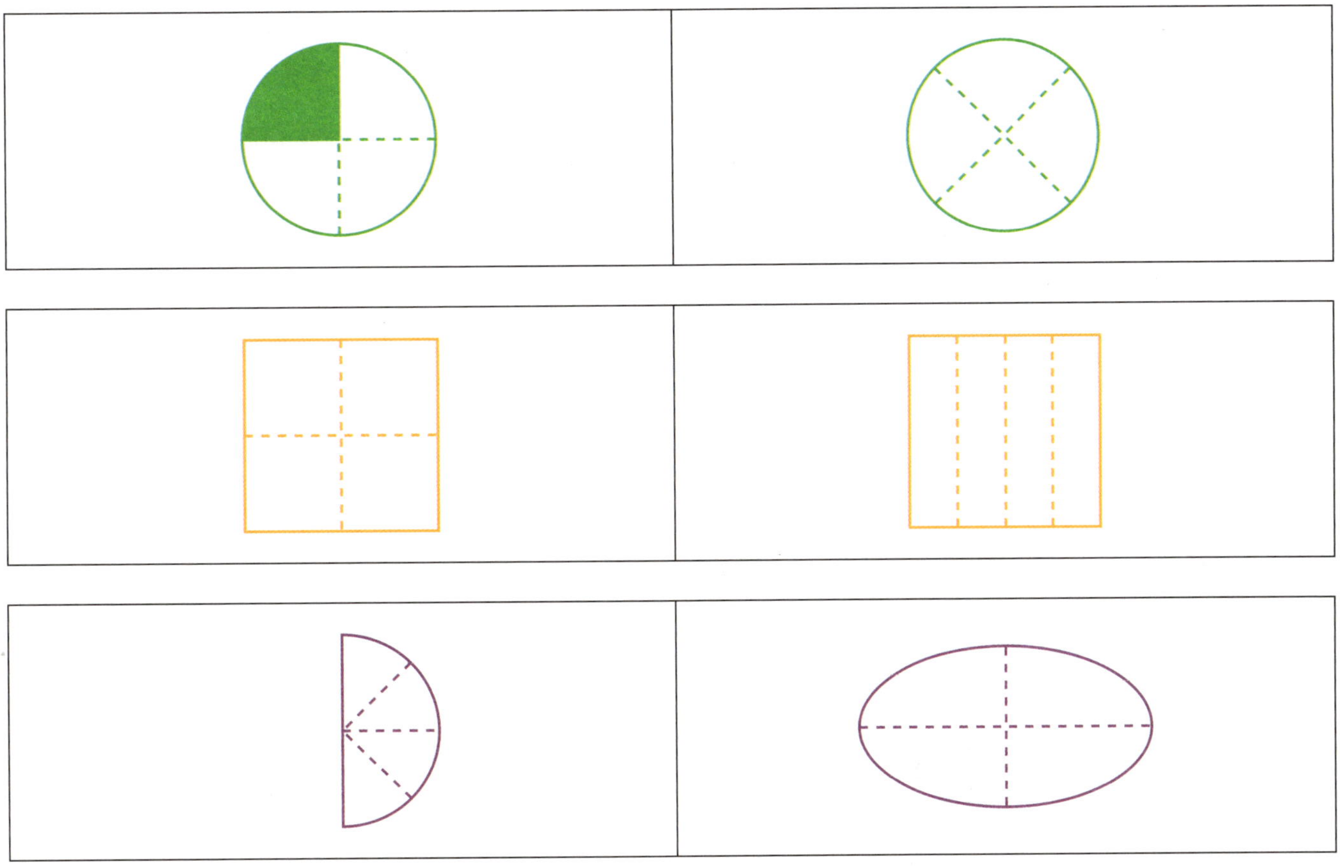

Learn Together

With your child, discuss halves and fourths when you are looking at other objects, particularly food that might be shared (crackers, pizza, cake, sandwiches).

Over and Over

Patterns repeat over and over.

Draw the part of each pattern that repeats over and over.

 ____________

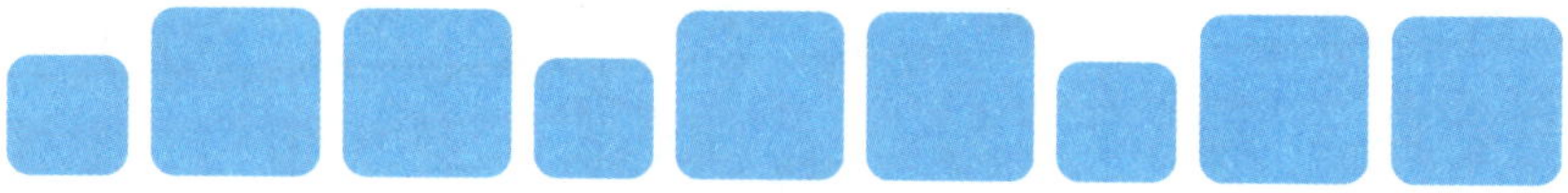 ____________

★☆☆★☆☆★☆☆★ ____________

ABA ABA ABA ABA ____________

Describe one of the patterns above.

____

Patterns can change by size, shape, colour, and direction.

Draw the part of each pattern that repeats.

 ______________________

 ____

ABB ABB ABB ABB ______________________

ABcD ABcD ABcD ABcD ______________________

Describe one of the patterns above.

____

Learn Together

With your child, use blocks with two or three different colours (or shapes) to create a repeating pattern. Discuss the pattern.

Colourful Patterns

Elsa uses her magic to make crystals. What patterns do you see?

Finish each of the patterns below by adding colour.

Choose 2 shapes and 2 colours to make a pattern.

Draw your pattern.

Now choose 3 shapes and 3 colours to make a pattern.

Draw your pattern.

Learn Together

Look for patterns in your home (tiles or wallpaper, or how the table is set: fork, plate, glass, fork, plate, glass). Encourage your child to describe the pattern and continue it.

Growing and Shrinking

Extend each pattern.

Circle if the pattern is **shrinking** or **growing**.

shrinking

growing

shrinking

growing

Extend each pattern.

Circle if the pattern is **shrinking** or **growing**.

5 10 15 20 25 30	____	shrinking growing
FFFFF FFFF FFF	____	shrinking growing
32 30 28 26 24 22	____	shrinking growing

Learn Together

With your child, create shrinking and growing patterns for each other to extend.

It All Adds Up

How many books does Olaf read?

$3 + 6 =$ ☐

$4 + 2 =$ ☐

$7 + 10 =$ ☐

$8 + 3 =$ ☐

$9 + 9 =$ ☐

$11 + 5 =$ ☐

$4 + 8 =$ ☐

$14 + 2 =$ ☐

Look at the 10-frames.

Write the addition sentences.

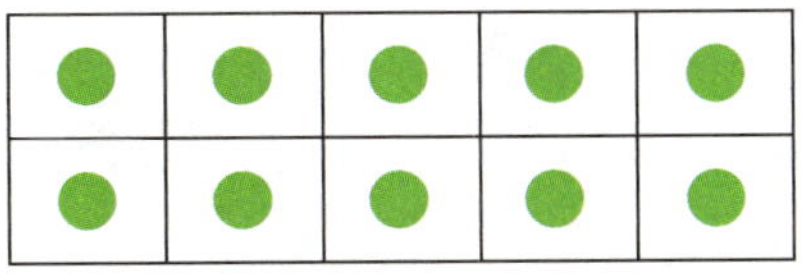 + 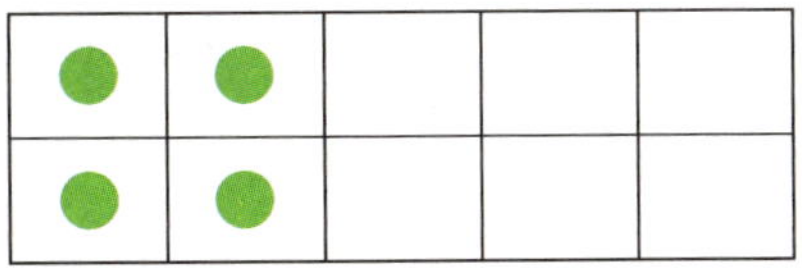

___ + ___ = ___

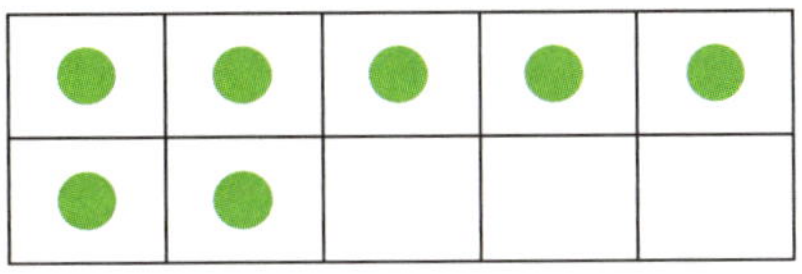 + 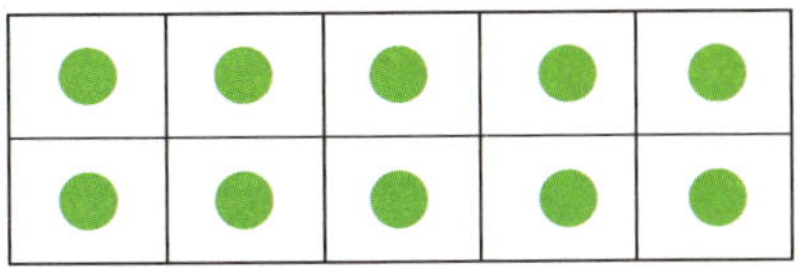

___ + ___ = ___

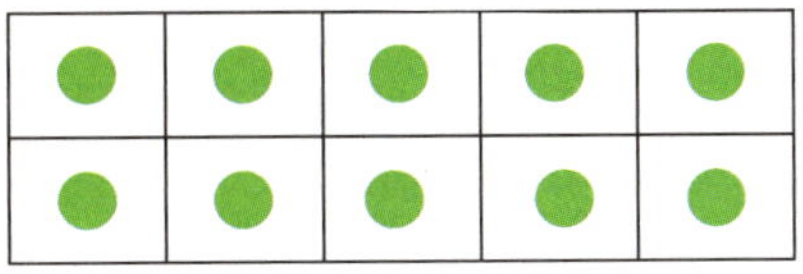 + 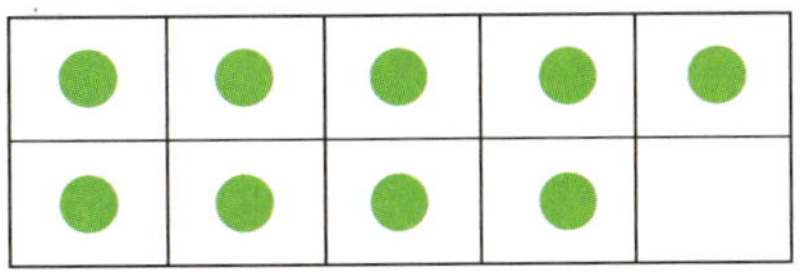

___ + ___ = ___

Learn Together

Use small objects to recreate the equations on page 92. Create other problems for your child to solve using the objects. Encourage them to record the problem using an **addition sentence**.

How Many?

Kristoff helps 19 villagers.

1 Kristoff and 19 villagers

is [ ]

Find each sum.

You can use counters to help you.

The **sum** is the answer to an addition sentence.

11 + 9 = [ ]

6 + 14 = [ ]

19 + 1 = [ ]

9 + 11 = [ ]

What do you notice about the sums?

___

Find each sum.

You can use counters to help you.

12 + 8 = ☐ 15 + 5 = ☐

3 + 17 = ☐ 5 + 15 = ☐

What do you notice about the sums?

____

Write another addition sentence that fits with the ones above.

Learn Together

Your child can use up to 20 counters or objects to show the same number in different ways (15 can be shown using 10 counters and 5 counters, 7 counters and 8 counters, 12 counters and 3 counters, and so on).

Adding Nothing

Read this addition story.

The 5 friends play a game. No one else is playing. How many friends are playing the game?

This addition story can be written as an addition sentence.

$5 + 0 = 5$

Find each sum.

$20 + 0 =$ ☐ $0 + 11 =$ ☐

$12 + 0 =$ ☐ $17 + 0 =$ ☐

What do you notice when you add **0** to a number?

____

How many people are in this picture?

No one joins them.

Write the addition sentence for this story.

☐ + ☐ = ☐

Find each sum.

$18 + 0 =$ ☐

$0 + 25 =$ ☐

$31 + 0 =$ ☐

$0 + 14 =$ ☐

$49 + 0 =$ ☐

$50 + 0 =$ ☐

Learn Together

Your child should begin to understand why a number remains the same when zero is added to it. Discuss what they notice about these addition sentences. Create other **addition stories** using these pictures.

Solve It!

When the friends work together, they can solve any problem!

How do you solve two-digit addition problems?

You can solve 10 + 14 using a 50-chart.

Find 14 on the 50-chart. Jump forward 10 to get 24.

1	2	3	4	5	6	7	8	9	10
11	12	13	14	15	16	17	18	19	20
21	22	23	24	25	26	27	28	29	30
31	32	33	34	35	36	37	38	39	40
41	42	43	44	45	46	47	48	49	50

You can also solve 10 + 14 by making friendly numbers.

10 + 14

10 + 10 + 4 = 24

So, 10 + 14 = 24

Find each sum.

13 + 10 = ☐ 15 + 10 = ☐

16 + 10 = ☐ 17 + 10 = ☐

20 + 10 = ☐ 20 + 13 = ☐

20 + 15 = ☐ 20 + 20 = ☐

20 + 21 = ☐ 20 + 22 = ☐

Learn Together

Your child may use various strategies to solve these problems, including using a 50-chart, interconnecting blocks, or counters on 10-frames. Discuss the strategies they are using.

Counting Yummy Carrots

Sven is very hungry!

There are 12 carrots.

Sven eats some carrots.

How many carrots are left?

Write the **subtraction sentence**.

____ − ____ = ____

____ − ____ = ____

Look at the 10-frames.

Write the subtraction sentences.

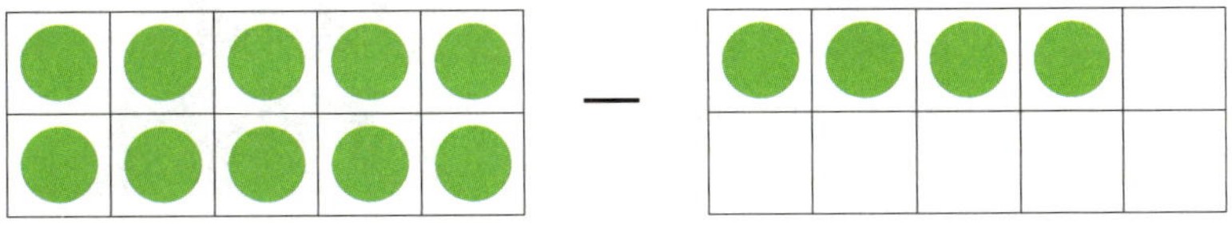

$\square - \square = \square$

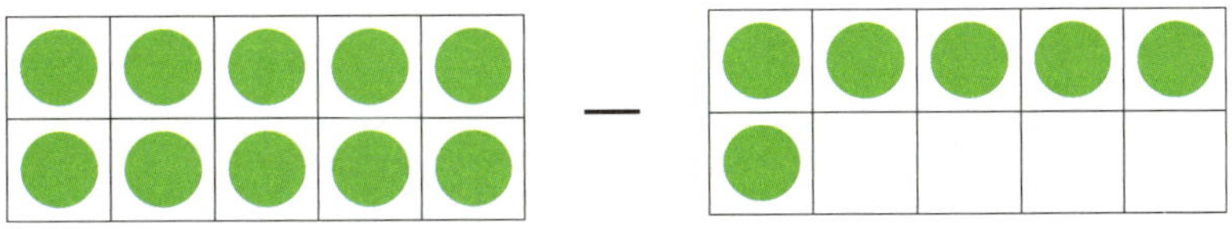

$\square - \square = \square$

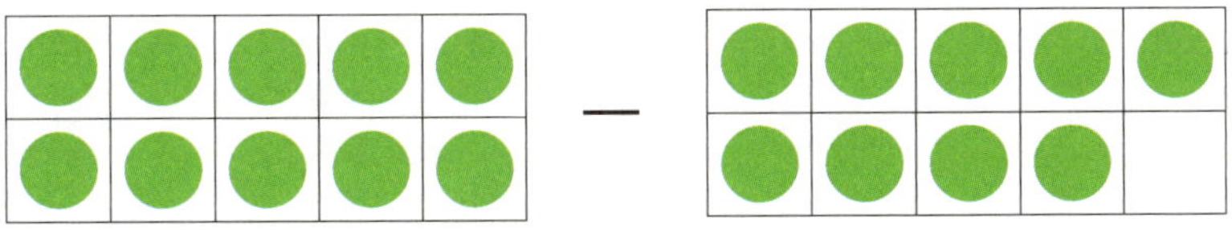

$\square - \square = \square$

Learn Together

Create other **subtraction sentences** for your child to solve by covering 10-frames with counters (buttons, blocks).

What's Left?

The 5 friends are together.

Then Olaf runs off.

How many are left?

$5 - 1 = \square$

Subtract to find each difference.

The **difference** is the answer to a subtraction sentence.

$9 - 1 = \square$

$7 - 3 = \square$

$14 - 1 = \square$

$8 - 3 = \square$

$18 - 4 = \square$

$12 - 4 = \square$

$17 - 4 = \square$

$16 - 4 = \square$

Anna, Elsa, and Kristoff walk together.

Anna and Kristoff lose Elsa.

How many friends are left?

3 − 1 = ☐

Subtract to find each difference.

18 − 2 = ☐

20 − 2 = ☐

18 − 3 = ☐

20 − 3 = ☐

18 − 4 = ☐

24 − 4 = ☐

18 − 5 = ☐

25 − 5 = ☐

Learn Together

Make subtraction part of everyday activities. How many bananas are left when we eat 1 for breakfast? When we clean 4 dirty dishes, how many dirty dishes are left?

Take Away Nothing!

Read this subtraction story.

The 5 friends stay together.

 $- 0 =$ 

Solve these subtraction sentences.

$18 - 0 =$ ☐ $10 - 0 =$ ☐

$11 - 0 =$ ☐ $17 - 0 =$ ☐

What do you notice when you subtract **0** from a number?

____

Solve these subtraction sentences.

Use counters or 10-frames to help you.

17 − 1 = ☐	16 − 5 = ☐
13 − 3 = ☐	12 − 3 = ☐
15 − 4 = ☐	19 − 6 = ☐
18 − 0 = ☐	11 − 1 = ☐
20 − 5 = ☐	14 − 4 = ☐
16 − 3 = ☐	18 − 5 = ☐
12 − 4 = ☐	15 − 0 = ☐

Learn Together

With your child, create a new **subtraction story** for the image on page 104 ("There are 5 friends, but Olaf and Sven wander away. Three friends remain.").

Cloudy Calculations

The monoliths are covered in misty clouds.

What can you add or subtract to change the first number into the final number?

The first one is done for you.

20	− 2 =	18	7		18
8		19	17		11
12		3	20		25
5		15	16		4

7		5	24		12
11		15	13		21
9		17	22		25
16		12	15		9
25		20	14		21
8		4	8		14
20		10	10		20

Learn Together

Your child can use 10-frames to picture each problem. If they need a hint, tell them to first figure out if the answer is increasing (addition) or decreasing (subtraction).

Joining Equal Groups

You **multiply** when you join equal groups.

Here are **4** groups of **2** crystals.

There are **8** crystals altogether.

$4 \times 2 = 8$

This is another way to show the word multiply.

Here are ______ groups of ______ crystals.

There are ______ crystals altogether.

Here are ____ groups of ____ crystals.

There are ____ crystals altogether.

____ × ____ = ____

Here are ____ groups of ____ crystals.

There are ____ crystals altogether.

____ × ____ = ____

Learn Together

As your child is being introduced to multiplication, they will still be counting the items within each group to reach a total. Using concrete objects to help them with multiplication is part of this early learning.

Let's Multiply

The Enchanted Forest is beautiful. There are many animals in the forest.

You can multiply to count how many.

There are **3** groups of **2** bunnies.

There are **6** bunnies all together.

$3 \times 2 = 6$

There are **2** groups of **3** ducklings.

$2 \times 3 =$ ☐

There are **6** groups of **2** ducklings.

$6 \times 2 =$ ☐

There are **5** groups of **2** ducklings.

$5 \times 2 =$ ☐

There are **3** groups of **3** bunnies.

$3 \times 3 =$ ☐

Learn Together

Provide your child with other simple scenarios to practise multiplying. Say, "Let's multiply as we set the table. We need 3 sets of 4: 4 plates, 4 knives, and 4 forks. 3 × 4 = 12.

Counting Groups

The Enchanted Forest is beautiful. Olaf counts the leaves on the trees.

Circle every group of **2** leaves.

Fill in the boxes.

$2 + 2 + 2 + 2 + 2 + \square = \square$

There are $\square$ groups of 2.

$\square \times 2 = \square$

There are $\square$ leaves.

Olaf counts more leaves!

How many leaves are there?

Circle every group of **3** leaves.

Fill in the boxes.

$3 + 3 + 3 + \square = \square$

There are $\square$ groups of 3.

$\square \times 3 = \square$

There are $\square$ leaves.

Learn Together

With your child, create other multiplication **arrays**. Encourage them to use 10-frames and counters to help them solve the problems.

Separating Equal Groups

You **divide** when you want to share a group in equal parts.

1 basket holds **4** loaves of bread.

How many baskets do you need for **8** loaves?

☐ baskets.

How many baskets do you need for **12** loaves?

☐ baskets.

How many baskets do you need for **16** loaves?

☐ baskets.

How many baskets do you need for **20** loaves?

☐ baskets.

How many baskets do you need for **24** loaves?

☐ baskets.

Learn Together

Your child is just being introduced to the concept of division. Help your child solve these problems. Provide them with counters to arrange into groups of 4.

Sharing is Division!

Anna has 12 chocolates.

Anna shares her chocolates with Elsa.

She can **divide** them equally to find out how many chocolates to give Elsa.

This is another way to show the word divide.

$12 \div 2 = 6$

Circle groups of chocolates to show each division sentence.

$12 \div 6 =$ ☐	
$12 \div 3 =$ ☐	
$12 \div 4 =$ ☐	

Learn Together

Use objects like beads to find the answers and create other problems to solve. The idea of sharing is a familiar one for children, and can help them understand how one group might be divided into smaller equal groups.

Measure It!

Who is taller, Olaf or Sven?

You can measure people and objects to find out exactly how tall they are.

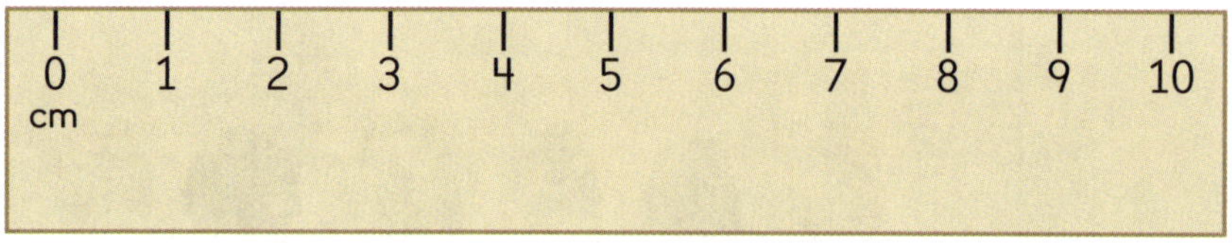

The symbol for a centimetre is **cm**.

This blue line is 3 cm long.

How long is this red line?

How long is this orange line?

Use a ruler to measure these items.

My thumb is about ________________ cm long.

My hand is about ________________ cm long.

My arm is about ________________ cm long.

My foot is about ________________ cm long.

My pencil is about ________________ cm long.

My favourite book is about ________________ cm long.

My favourite toy is about ________________ cm long.

Learn Together

If your child is using a ruler for the first time, they will need help to understand how to use it. They can measure other items using a ruler or tape measure. Discuss the terms *length*, *width*, and *height* and how they differ.

Hold It!

Which containers
hold about the **same**?

Circle the objects in each row
that hold about the **same**.

Estimate how many glasses of water each container will hold.

Circle the container that holds the **most**.

Container	Estimate	Actual Measurement
pitcher 		
pot 		
pan 		

Learn Together Provide your child with a glass and the other containers to help them estimate, and then measure how much each will hold. Find other containers around your home and create a **chart** like the one above.

Heavy or Light?

It's Kristoff and Sven!

Who do you think
is the **heaviest**?

Circle the object in each pair that is **heavier**.

You can use a pan balance to compare the mass of two objects.

If you put two objects on a pan balance, how do you know which one is lighter?

Learn Together

Help your child compare the mass of objects using a pan balance, or a kitchen or bathroom scale. Note that your child may not yet have been introduced to units of measurement for mass.

How Big?

Estimate the number of squares that cover this picture.

Now count the number of squares that cover the picture.

You figured out the **area** of the picture.

Area is the amount of space inside of a shape.

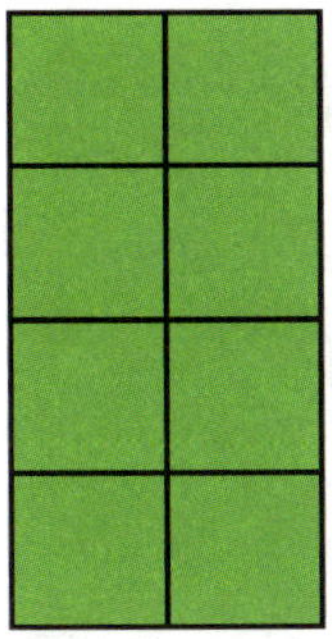

Estimate the area of this rectangle. ☐

Count the squares.

The area is ☐ squares.

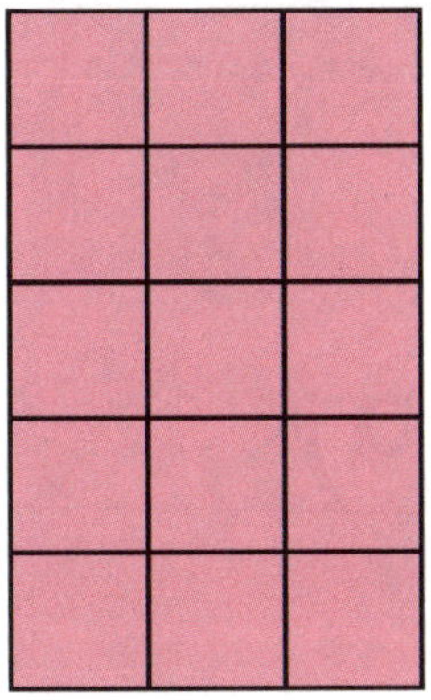

Estimate the area of this rectangle. ☐

Count the squares.

The area is ☐ squares.

Estimate the area of this rectangle. ☐

Count the squares.

The area is ☐ squares.

Learn Together

Work with your child to find the area of other objects. Use different items to cover the surface (cubes, blocks) and compare the area of each surface.

Counting the Days

The friends travel for many days.

Arrange these in order from **shortest** to **longest**.

month **week** **year** **day**

How many months are in **1** year? ☐

How many days are in **1** week? ☐

Some months have 31 days.

Some months have 30 days.

February has 28 days, except every 4 years it has 29.

Put the month and numbers (or dates) on this calendar.

Month: ____________________

Sunday	Monday	Tuesday	Wednesday	Thursday	Friday	Saturday

Put a star on today's date.

How many days until the end of the month? ☐

Learn Together

Help your child complete the calendar above for the current month. Plan activities using the calendar. Discuss how many days, or weeks, are left until certain events will occur.

Time Enough

A clock tells the time.

Match each clock to the correct time.

8:45

8:15

8:00

8:30

Show the time you wake up.

:

Show the time you eat lunch.

:

Show the time you go to bed.

:

Learn Together

Your child is just beginning to understand the concept of time. Practise telling time together and talk about time ("It's five o'clock. Do you want to help me get dinner ready?" "It's 7:30, half an hour to your bedtime.").

Shaping Up

The friends see many shapes in Arendelle.

What shapes do you see in this picture?

Complete the table below.

Shape	Draw the Shape	Number of Sides
square		
rectangle		
triangle		
circle		

Pentagons have **5** sides.

Trace this pentagon.

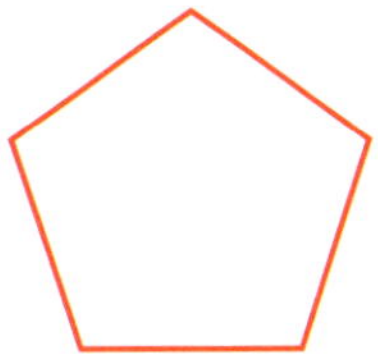

Now, draw your own pentagon.

Circle the pentagons.

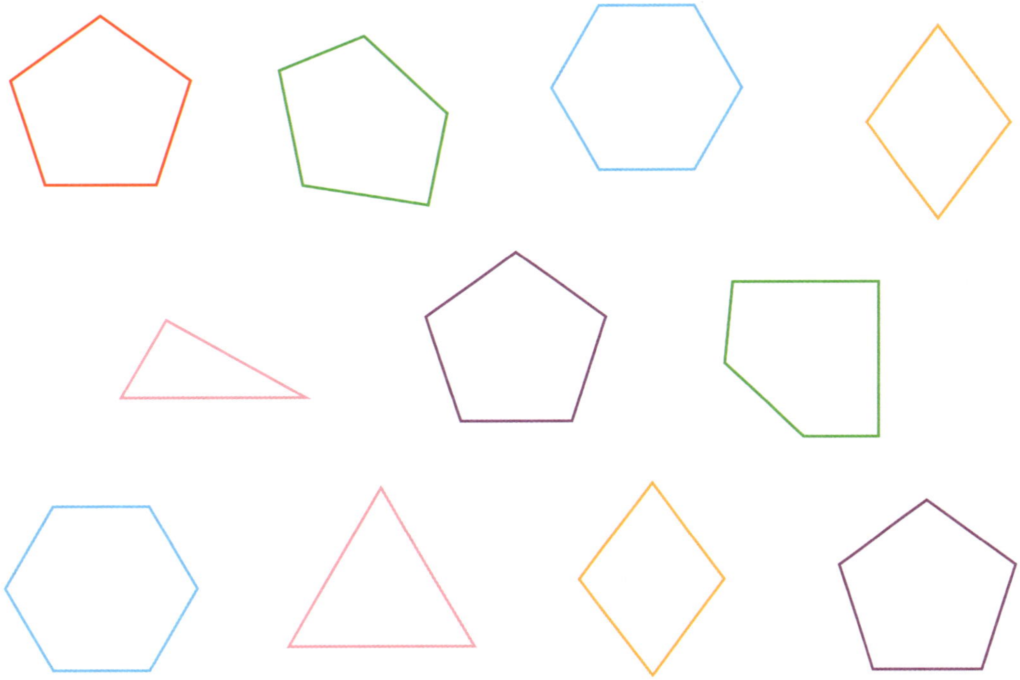

Learn Together

With your child, discuss and compare these shapes.

Many Sides

Hexagons have **6** sides.

Trace this hexagon.

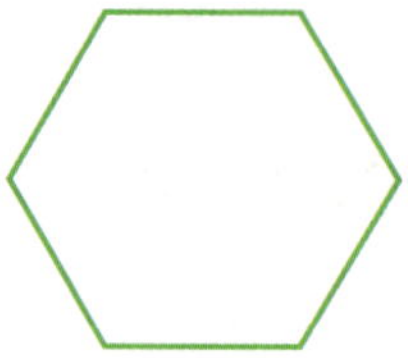

Now, draw your own hexagon.

Circle the hexagons.

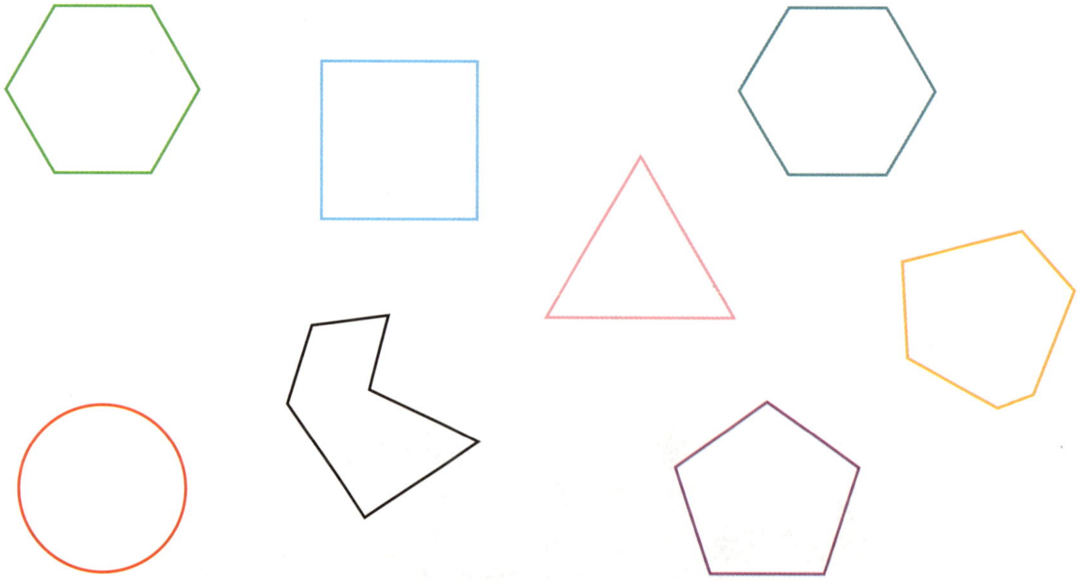

Octagons have **8** sides.

Trace this octagon.

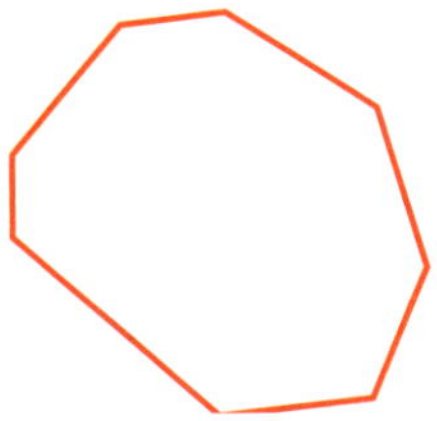

Now, draw your own octagon.

Circle the octagons.

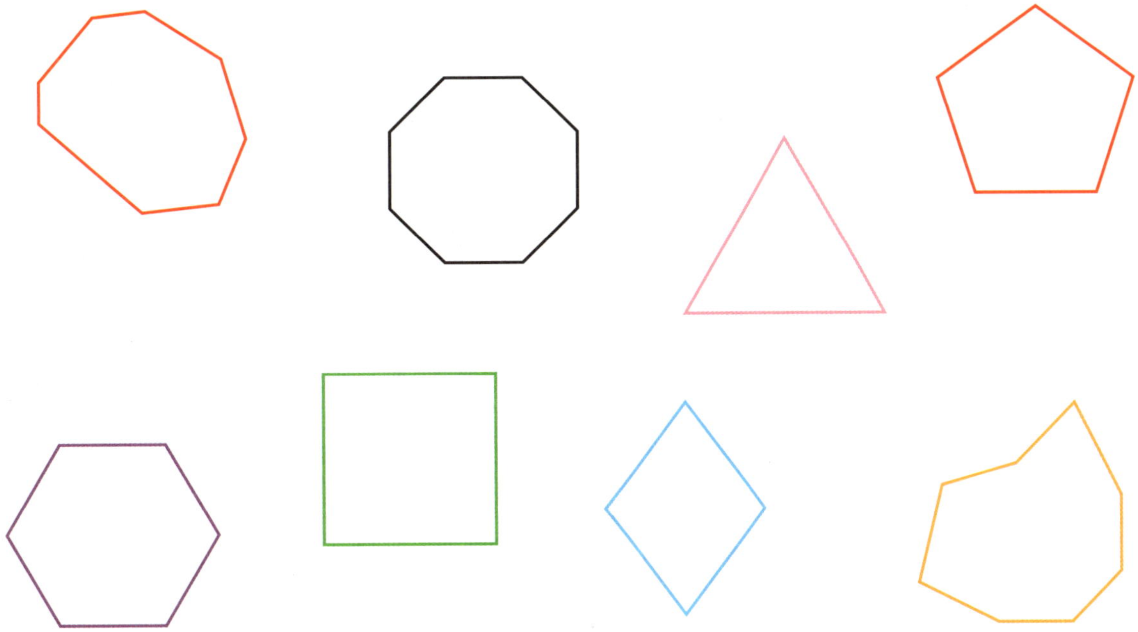

Learn Together

With your child, look for shapes in your home. Count the sides. Sort the shapes using a table like the one on page 164. Your child can draw the shape in the first column.

3-D Objects

Each of these drums is a 3-D object called a **cylinder**.

Use these words to write the name of each 3-D object below.

cube **cone** **cylinder** **sphere**

 ____________

 ____________

 ____________

 ____________

Use the clues to answer these riddles.

All my faces are the same and I have 8 vertices.

What am I? ______________________

I have one vertex and can roll.

What am I? ______________________

I have flat faces and can be stacked.

What am I? ______________________

I have no vertices and can roll.

What am I? ______________________

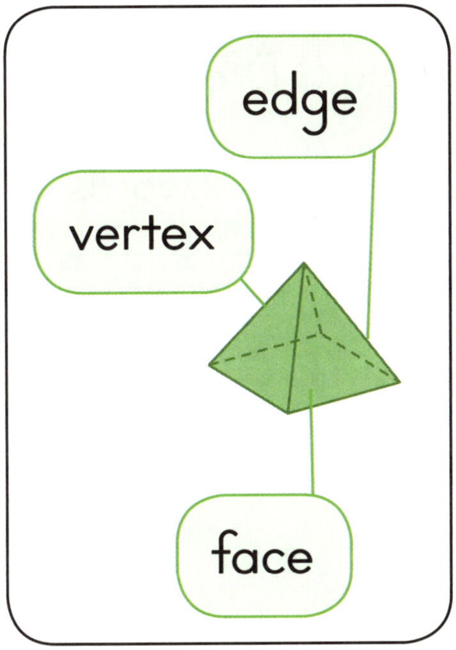

Learn Together

Help your child create other riddles for 3-D objects. Your child can create 3-D objects using modelling clay or other materials. They can describe and label the objects.

In 3-D

What 3-D objects do you see in this picture?

Pyramids and **prisms** are also 3-D objects.

Use these words to name each 3-D object below.

triangular prism **cone** **pyramid**

rectangular prism

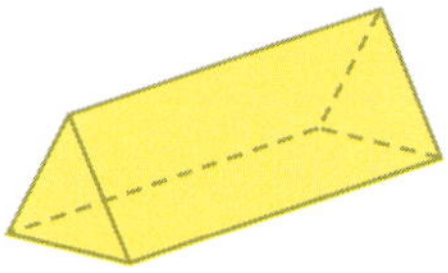 ______________________

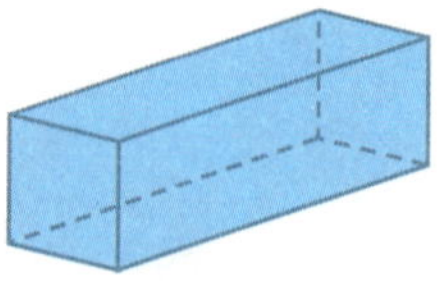 ______________________

 ______________________

Use the clues to answer these riddles.

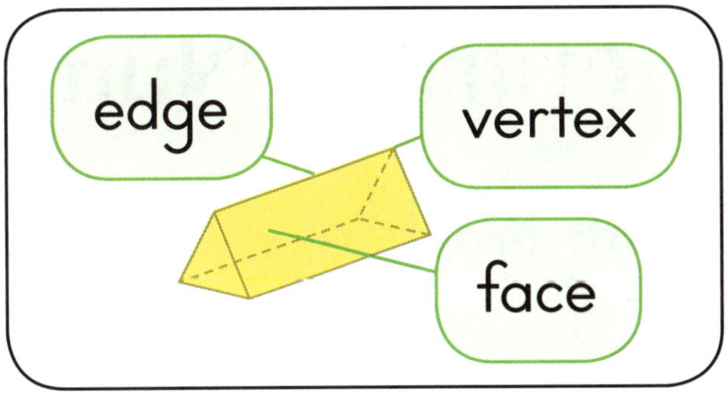

I have six faces and can stack.

What am I? ______________________________

I have one vertex and can roll.

What am I? ______________________________

I have two triangular faces and three rectangular faces.

What am I? ______________________________

Write another riddle for one 3-D object.

____

Learn Together Talk about how some shapes can roll and some shapes can stack (and some can do both). Use blocks or other objects to experiment to find out which 3-D objects are best for stacking and rolling.

Picturing Numbers

A **bar graph** uses bars to show **data**.

Anna's Chocolates

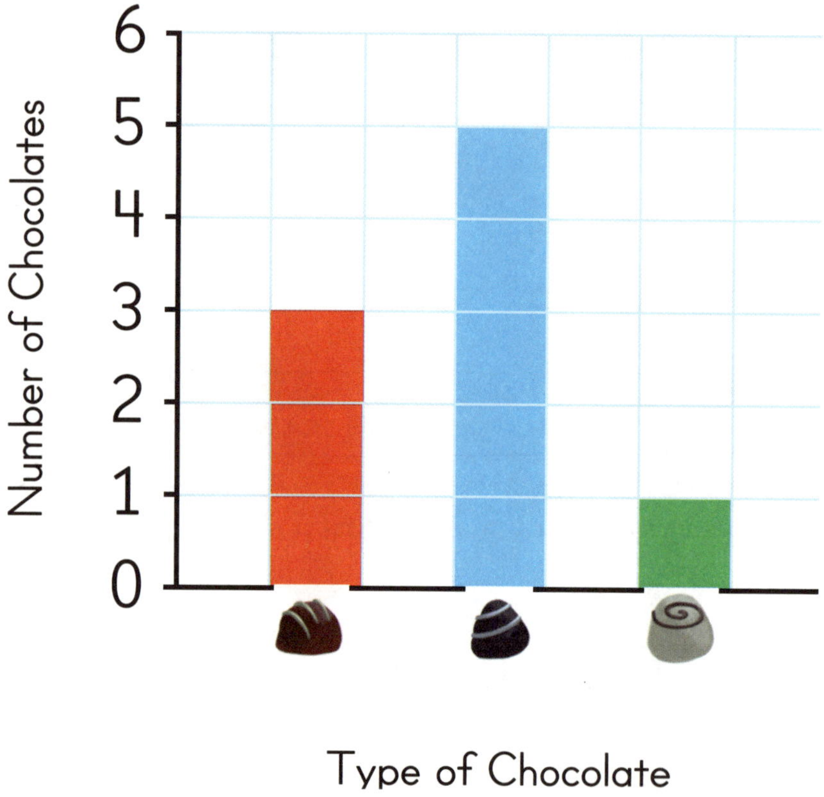

Circle the chocolate Anna has the most of.

Olaf has some balloons.

Read the bar graph.

Olaf's Balloon Collection

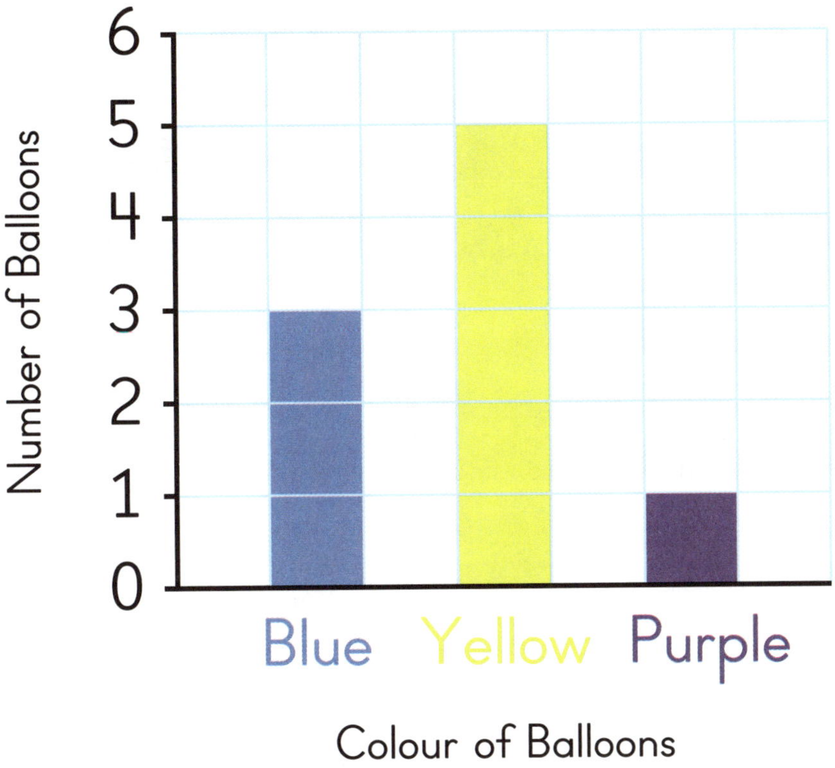

What colour balloon does Olaf have the **most** of? ____________________

What colour balloon does Olaf have the **least** of? ____________________

Learn Together

Help your child read the bar graph. Ask your child questions about the bar graph. Example: "How many yellow balloons does Olaf have?"

Graph Up

Elsa, Anna, and Kristoff go sledding down the hill.

The number of times each friend goes sledding is on this **line plot**.

A **line plot** uses an x to show how many times something happened.

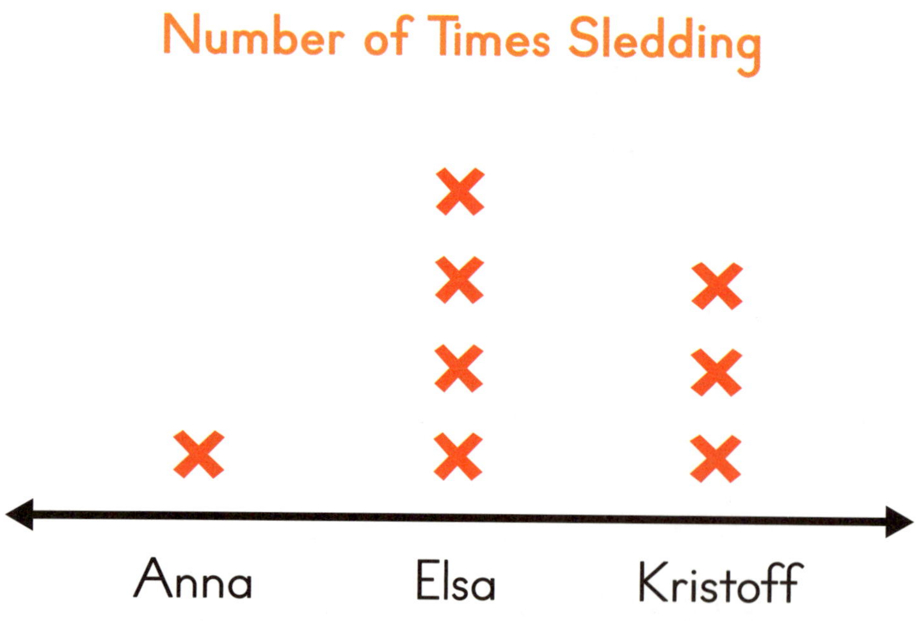

Which friend goes sledding **five** times?

____

Create a line plot.
Show the favourite ice cream flavours of your family or friends.

Favourite Ice Cream Flavours

What does your line plot tell you? ________________________________

____

Learn Together

Help your child create other line plots. Ask them questions about the most and least popular choices.

What's Next?

As your child completes the topics in this book, extend their learning with some of the following activities.

Letter Recognition

- Help your child arrange objects in alphabetical order.
- Together, sort books into alphabetical order on your child's bookshelf. Decide whether it will be alphabetical by title or author's last name.
- At the store, encourage your child to look at how the spices are organized (usually in alphabetical order). Name a spice for them to find. Take turns finding spices you each name.
- Your child is surrounded by environmental print. Examples include signs, labels, maps, and advertising. Encourage them to read environmental print, praising their growing reading ability.

Word Knowledge

- Your child can highlight word patterns they see in these activities (such as the long *o* sound in *road, boat, soap*; adding *-ed* to some verbs to make the past tense). They can begin a word knowledge notebook for word patterns and word families.
- As your child's reading skills develop, they will notice many exceptions to general rules (the *ei* in *eight* makes a long *a* sound, not a long *e* sound; past tense of *swim* is *swam*, not *swimmed*). Challenge them to add these rules and exceptions to their word knowledge notebook.
- Use fridge magnets or flash cards to create word families (short vowel: *-ad, -at, -et, ed*; long vowel: *-ape, -aid, -eet, -eed*). Your child can experiment with adding consonants to make words (dad, pad, mad, sad; deed, seed, feed).
- Create a three-column chart for nouns—person, place, thing. Give your child a minute to list as many nouns as they can think of.
- Together, play a game of charades. Take turns acting out a verb.

Comprehension

- As you read or watch shows, ask your child questions to help them make predictions and inferences.
- Encourage your child's questions about stories and nonfiction text.
- Use wordless picture books to help your child practise making inferences and drawing conclusions.
- To practise making inferences, play Paper Bag Mysteries. Add some clues about a familiar character to a paper bag. Your child can remove the clues one by one and start to make inferences about who the character is.
- The classic game of Twenty Questions requires your child to make inferences.
- As you read the title of a book, ask: "What do you think the story is about? Who is the main character? Do you think the story will be happy, sad, or something else? Why?"
- Your child will still need support identifying the main idea. As you watch movies together, discuss the main idea. Challenge them to summarize the movie.
- Pictures help your child make sense of text. Encourage your child to examine the pictures closely to understand what has happened, where a story is set, or how characters are feeling.

Writing

- Create a mystery message together for someone else to read—omit the first letter of each word.
- Create sentence starters for your child to finish. ("I want a ____. Do you want to go to the ________? I love ________.")
- Create a digital photo album together, with photos of your child's life. They can write simple captions.
- With your child, write stories, lists, letters, poems, and other texts.
- Write notes to one another and leave them in secret places.
- Together, create a treasure map for your child to follow.
- Your child can write labels or captions for their drawings.
- As your child writes using various verb tenses, encourage them to say the sentence to figure out form and spelling. Look for patterns that can help them (ending some verbs with *-ed*) and for exceptions to rules (ate/eat; got/get; went/go) that they can add to their word knowledge notebook.
- What kind of superheroes would you and your child like to be? Draw pictures of yourselves as superheroes. Label the parts of your costumes and write captions for your pictures.

What's Next?

Number Sense

- Using 100 small objects, make number groups (40 objects, 60 objects). Your child can write the number and the word for that number.
- Create 10-frame boxes to help your child count objects. Create a hundreds chart and provide your child with 100 counters (buttons, beads) to cover it to help them with addition and subtraction.
- Invite your child to help you cook and bake. Point out how many recipes use fractions. Can they figure out how much of each ingredient is needed?
- Count backwards from 100 together, pausing now and then to let your child fill in the number.

Collecting and Using Data

- Play games that include an element of probability (any game that includes dice, spinners, or cards).
- Discuss the outcome of events using phrases such as *unlikely*, *certain*, and *impossible*.
- Look for graphs and tables as you read nonfiction texts together. Ask questions about the graphs and tables.

Patterns

- Encourage your child to sort objects, such as toys, by providing them with bins or other containers. Talk about the rules they are using to sort. ("All of the red toys went in the red bin. Are you sorting by colour?")
- Your child can sort their laundry as they put it away. What rule will they use?
- Mix some objects into a bin (pens, toys, spoons). What rule will your child use to sort the objects?
- As you take out or put away seasonal decorations, allow your child to help sort the objects (by colour, purpose, material, size, and so on).
- Look for patterns in nature and around your home.
- Give your child objects to create patterns with (blocks, buttons, school supplies, toys).
- Create a pattern and ask your child to add to it. Ask your child to create a pattern for you to finish.

Addition and Subtraction

- With your child, create a number line from zero to 100. Give them groups of objects to add and subtract.
- Play games involving skip counting ("hide and seek" with the searcher counting to 100 by 2s). Skip count by 2s, 5s, and 10s together.
- Use connecting blocks to make counting cubes (1s, 10s, and 100s) for solving problems. ("If I have 32 blocks and 23 blocks, how many blocks do I have altogether?").
- Look for natural sets in your home that can be used for problems involving multiplication and division (two cases of juice boxes; 12 cans of soup).
- When you shop, provide opportunities to multiply and divide. Say, "If we need three apples a day for five days, how many apples do we need? This pizza has 12 pieces, and 4 people will eat it. How many pieces does each person get?"

Measurement

- Encourage your child to compare the length, width, or height of various items. Ask: "Is your glass taller than a pencil? Is your book wider than a favourite toy?"
- Use your cellphone to look for geocaches in your neighbourhood. Your child will enjoy the adventure of finding hidden objects as they learn how to follow directions and navigate.
- With your child, talk about the timing of events. "Next Wednesday, we'll go swimming at seven o'clock. But that means we'll need to eat half an hour earlier. What time should we eat?"

Geometry

- Look for 3-D objects in your home, noting their shapes (cans are cylinders). Your child can draw and label the objects and shapes.
- Look for shapes as you take a walk in your neighbourhood. ("That door is a rectangle. The window is a square.")
- Look for 3-D objects in your neighbourhood. If possible, let your child examine and touch all the sides.
- Look for maps as you are out with your child—in shopping malls, parks, and bus stations. Examine the maps together.
- Use position words to describe the location of places.

Glossary

100-chart a table that displays the numbers from 1 to 100 (or 0 to 99). This chart can be a useful tool for your child when skip counting, adding, or subtracting.

10-frames two-by-five rectangle frames used to help teach counting. Counters are placed to illustrate numbers less than or equal to ten.

addition sentence a number sentence or equation used to express addition (4 + 1 = 5).

addition stories one or more statements that illustrate a math addition equation. For example, the equation 2 + 2 = 4 could be told as a story about two children who are joined by two friends.

alphabetical order to arrange words according to the order of letters in the alphabet.

arrays to arrange items in rows or columns to make it easier to count or calculate totals.

background knowledge what your child knows of the world—information that can help them as they read. As they read stories, they connect to that knowledge to help them make sense of text. Your child will use background knowledge to make predictions, make inferences, and draw conclusions.

chart (or table) a graphic organizer used to sort and organize information in ways that make it easier to read, compare it, and understand it.

compound word a word composed of two or more smaller words (background). Your child can sometimes use their knowledge of the smaller words to figure out the meaning of the compound word.

consonant blends two or more consonants that work together in a word, where each consonant can be distinctly heard (the *s* in *snake* or the *ft* in *raft*).

context the words or text surrounding an unfamiliar word that can be used to help clarify the meaning of that word.

contractions words created by joining two words using an apostrophe to replace the missing letters (don't, I'm, you're).

digraphs two consonants working together in a word to make one sound (the *sh* in *shake* or the *ck* in *block*).

drawing conclusions to make decisions about or evaluations of the events or characters in stories. This reading strategy supports your child's understanding of texts, but also requires them to apply critical thinking skills that are still developing.

estimating to use your understanding of numbers to make an educated guess at an answer to a problem.

fact true information that can be proven or supported. To become a critical reader and thinker, your child will need to differentiate between facts and opinions.

homophone words that sound the same but are spelled differently (to/two/too). It is natural when your child writes for them to still be spelling homophones incorrectly.

make predictions to form an educated guess about what will happen next. This strategy supports your child's understanding of texts.

Glossary

making connections a reading strategy that requires your child to use their background knowledge; this strategy supports your child's understanding of texts. There are three types of connections (text to self, text to text, and text to world).

making inferences to use clues in the text to "read between the lines." This reading strategy requires your child to use their critical thinking skills as well as their background knowledge and understanding of texts.

number line a line showing numbers along it, placed in order. Number lines can help your child as they add, subtract, or think about how one number is related to another (3 comes before 6, 10 is 9 numbers away from 1).

opinion a personal statement or belief. For example, blue is the best colour.

plural words words that indicate there is more than one of something. There are rules, and exceptions to those rules, to follow when making a word plural (baby/babies; child/children; person/people). Your child is just learning these rules as they spell, but will probably already be following the rules when speaking.

prefix letters added to the beginning of a word to change its meaning (return, undone).

probability the chance or likelihood of something happening. Help your child predict the outcome of events (ranging from *impossible* to *certain*) as an introduction to this math concept.

regrouping forming new groups, usually by arranging the ones and tens (or, in higher grades, hundreds and thousands) to understand the total and aid in making calculations.

silent letters letters in a word you do not hear when spoken (*k* in *knife*, *b* in *comb*). Your child is at a stage when they will spell many words as they sound, and not add the silent letters. Encourage them to think about word patterns or families, where appropriate (know, knowledge; when, where, what) or to make up memory aids to remember the spelling ("*B* sure to comb your hair every day.").

skip counting to count in increments other than one (2, 4, 6, 8, 10). Your child will be skip counting by 2s, 5s, and 10s.

story elements characters, setting, and plot are the features of a story. When your child can identify story elements, they develop their understanding and appreciation of the story.

subtraction sentence a number sentence or equation used to express subtraction (4 – 1 + 3).

subtraction stories one or more statements that illustrate a math subtraction equation. For example, the equation 4 – 2 = 2 could be told as a story about four children who are playing, but two friends leave.

suffix letters added to the end of a word to change its meaning (smaller).

verb tenses the varying form of the verb that expresses a time frame—past, present, or future.

verbs action words; note that the spelling rules for verbs can be complex, particularly irregular verbs, which take unusual forms depending on how they are used with other words or in other tenses (eat/ate, am/are/is—for *to be*, go/went, swim/swam).

word ending the letters at the end of a word that form a sound or make the word part of a word family. Your child is using common word endings to help them read new words (fight/right/might; flow/blow/know); knowing how one of these words is pronounced, helps them know how to pronounce other words with the same ending.

word families a group of words related in some way. For example, they begin or end with the same sound (*bed, fed, red* are part of the *-ed* word family).

Answers

Letter Recognition
A Magical Alphabet
Elsa and Anna are sisters.
Elsa has a magical power.
She can freeze things and create snow and ice with her hands!
Fill in the missing capital letters below.
A B C D E F G H I J K L M
N O P Q R S T U V W X Y Z
2

Fill in the missing lowercase letters below.
a b c d e f g h i j k l m
n o p q r s t u v w x y z
3

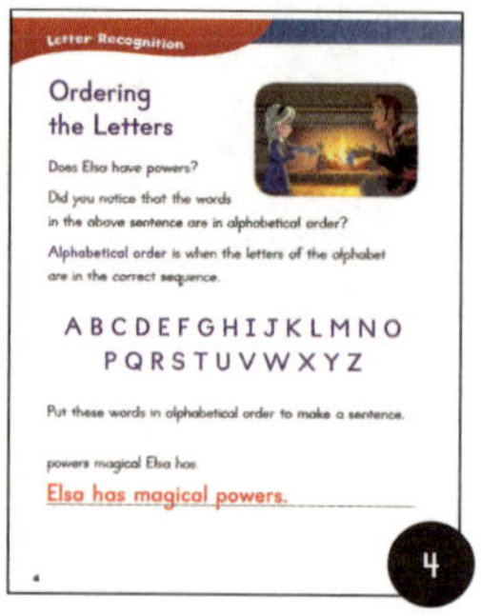
Letter Recognition
Ordering the Letters
Does Elsa have powers?
Did you notice that the words in the above sentence are in alphabetical order?
Alphabetical order is when the letters of the alphabet are in the correct sequence.
A B C D E F G H I J K L M N O
P Q R S T U V W X Y Z
Put these words in alphabetical order to make a sentence.
powers magical Elsa has
Elsa has magical powers.
4

Unlock the order of these letters.
Put each group of letters in alphabetical order.
The first one has been done for you.
B D A — A B D
A K T — A K T
d h f o — d f h o
z d r f — d f r z
U x j q — j q U x
h Y O S — h O S Y
l r q B — B l q r
W j D k — D j k W
5

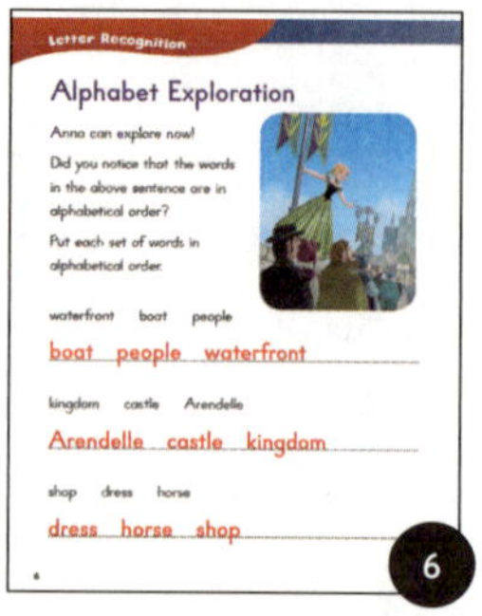
Letter Recognition
Alphabet Exploration
Anna can explore now!
Did you notice that the words in the above sentence are in alphabetical order?
Put each set of words in alphabetical order.
waterfront boat people
boat people waterfront
kingdom castle Arendelle
Arendelle castle kingdom
shop dress horse
dress horse shop
6

Hans charming prince
charming Hans prince
snow Elsa queen
Elsa queen snow
gates love Anna
Anna gates love
7

Letter Recognition
Lets Get Ready!
Elsa needs to get ready for her coronation.
Put these words in alphabetical order.
summer coronation room
coronation room summer
gloves scepter orb
gloves orb scepter
hall dance magic
dance hall magic
8

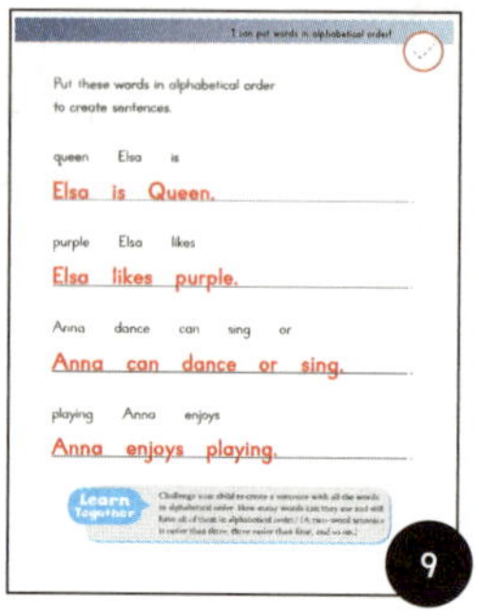
Put these words in alphabetical order to create sentences.
queen Elsa is
Elsa is Queen.
purple Elsa likes
Elsa likes purple.
Anna dance can sing or
Anna can dance or sing.
playing Anna enjoys
Anna enjoys playing.
9

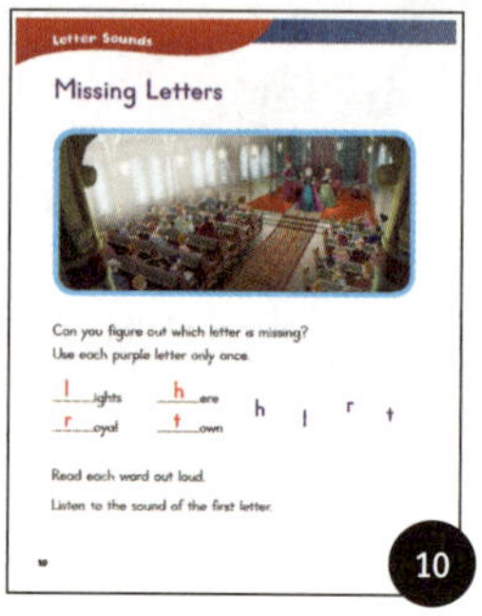
Letter Sounds
Missing Letters
Can you figure out which letter is missing?
Use each purple letter only once.
l ights h ere
r oyal t own
Read each word out loud.
Listen to the sound of the first letter.
10

Add the missing letters.
It's t ime for Elsa's coronation.
Elsa will become queen h ere in the main h all.
Many people wait in l ine to see r oyalty.
Read each sentence out loud.
Listen to the letter sounds.
11

Letter Sounds

More Missing Letters

Can you figure out which letter is missing?

sister dance ballroom walk

d s b w

Read each word out loud.

Listen to the sound of the first letter.

12

I can recognize consonant sounds!

Add the missing letters.

d s b w

Anna and Hans spend time at the ball

Hans asks Anna if she would like to dance.

They laugh and walk together.

It is love at first sight.

Hans asks Anna if she will marry him.

Anna is happy. She says yes!

Read each sentence out loud.

Listen to the letter sounds.

Learn Together

13

Letter Sounds

Magical Frozen Letters

Some letters are frozen.

Can you figure out which letter is missing?

Use each purple letter only once.

party night family magic

n m f p

Read each word out loud.

Listen to the sound of the first letter.

14

I can recognize consonant sounds!

Add the missing letters. n m f p

Anna and Hans ask Elsa to bless their marriage.

Elsa does not give her permission.

Elsa is firm. Anna feels upset.

Anna accidentally pulls off Elsa's glove.

Elsa flees the castle as her magic spills out.

Read each sentence out loud.

Listen to the letter sounds.

Learn Together

15

Letter Sounds

A Chilly End

The townspeople know about Elsa's powers.

Add the missing letter to the end of each word.

Use each purple letter only once.

map loom always from

p s m m

Listen to the sound of the last letter.

16

I can recognize consonant sounds!

Add the missing letter to the end of each word.

p s m k

The kingdom is in an uproar as ice spreads.

Anna finally understands why Elsa keeps to herself.

Anna sets out to find Elsa.

She wants to bring Elsa back to thaw out the kingdom.

Anna leaves to go up the mountain.

Read each sentence out loud.

Listen to the letter sounds.

Learn Together

17

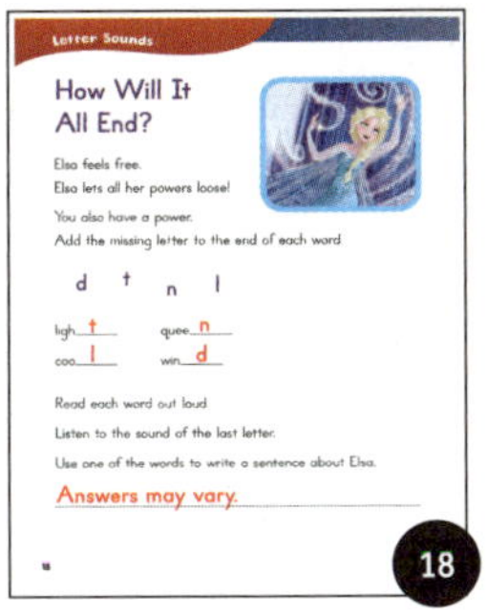
Letter Sounds

How Will It All End?

Elsa feels free.

Elsa lets all her powers loose!

You also have a power.

Add the missing letter to the end of each word.

d t n l

light queen cool wind

Read each word out loud.

Listen to the sound of the last letter.

Use one of the words to write a sentence about Elsa.

Answers may vary.

18

I can recognize consonant sounds!

Add the missing letter to the end of each word.

Hint: If two letters are missing in a word, it is the same letter.

d n t l

Elsa climbs high up the mountain.

Elsa uses her powers to build an amazing ice palace.

She feels like the person she is meant to be!

She knows it will be lonely in her ice palace.

At long last, Elsa knows she will be free!

Read each sentence out loud.

Listen to the letter sounds.

Learn Together

19

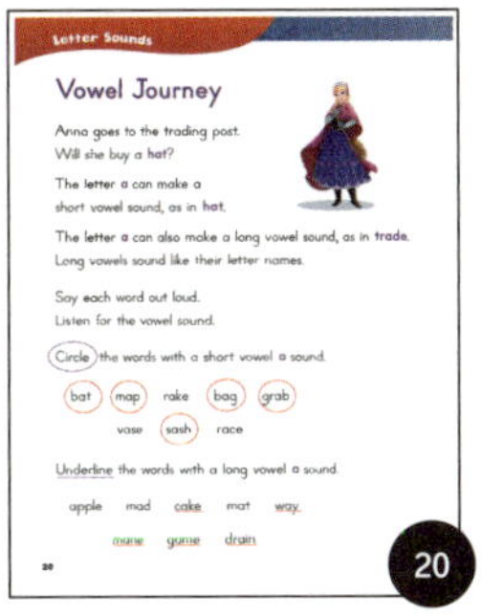
Letter Sounds

Vowel Journey

Anna goes to the trading post.

Will she buy a hat?

The letter a can make a short vowel sound, as in hat.

The letter a can also make a long vowel sound, as in trade.

Long vowels sound like their letter names.

Say each word out loud.

Listen for the vowel sound.

Circle the words with a short vowel a sound.

bat map rake bag grab vase sash race

Underline the words with a long vowel a sound.

apple mad cake mat way mane game drain

20

I can recognize vowel sounds!

Anna meets Kristoff and Sven at the trading post.

The letter e can make a short vowel sound, as in Sven.

The letter e can also make a long vowel sound, as in meet.

Circle the words with a short vowel e sound.

bed bee jet hen get bead feet red

Underline the words with a long vowel e sound.

fed leaf met seal meal set we test

Learn Together

21

Answers

Letter Sounds

Bit or Bite

The letter i can make a short vowel sound, as in mitt.

The letter i can also make a long vowel sound, as in ice.

Say each word out loud. Listen for the vowel sound.

Circle the words that have a short vowel i sound.

gift bit fine time side if king

Underline the words that have a long vowel i sound.

I pin vine fire fish bite it line

22

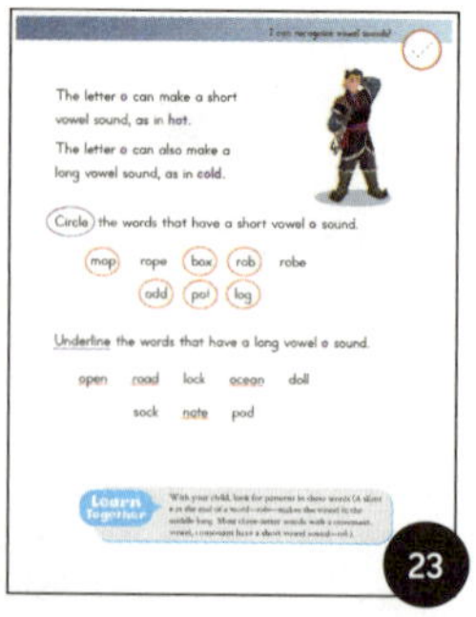

The letter o can make a short vowel sound, as in hot.

The letter o can also make a long vowel sound, as in cold.

Circle the words that have a short vowel o sound.

mop rope box rob robe odd pot log

Underline the words that have a long vowel o sound.

open road lock ocean doll sock note pod

23

Letter Sounds

Cut to the Cute

The new friends travel together.

The letter u can make a short vowel sound, as in uphill.

The letter u can also make a long vowel sound, as in use.

Say each word out loud. Listen for the vowel sound.

Circle the words that have a short vowel u sound.

cut rescue hut mug plum truck sun music

Underline the words that have a long vowel u sound.

duck cube use cute unite bug unicorn

24

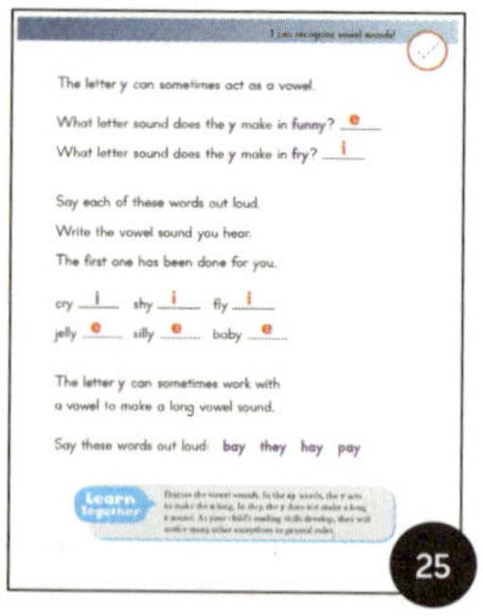

The letter y can sometimes act as a vowel.

What letter sound does the y make in funny? e

What letter sound does the y make in fry? i

Say each of these words out loud. Write the vowel sound you hear. The first one has been done for you.

cry i shy i fly i jelly e silly e baby e

The letter y can sometimes work with a vowel to make a long vowel sound.

Say these words out loud: boy they hay pay

25

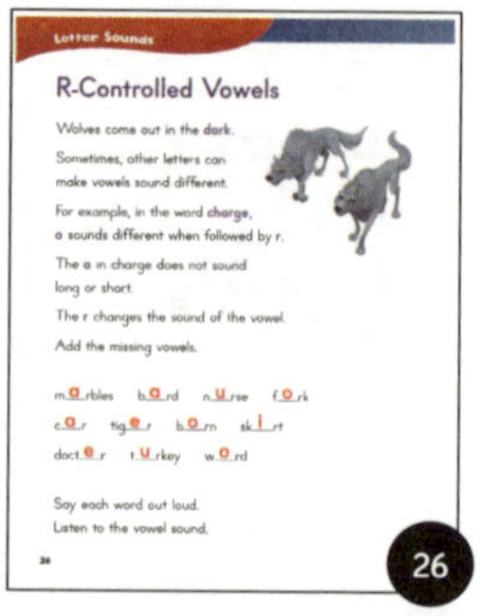

Letter Sounds

R-Controlled Vowels

Wolves come out in the dark.

Sometimes, other letters can make vowels sound different.

For example, in the word charge, a sounds different when followed by r.

The a in charge does not sound long or short.

The r changes the sound of the vowel.

Add the missing vowels.

m a rbles b i rd n u rse f o rk c a r tig e r h o rn sk i rt doct o r t u rkey w o rd

Say each word out loud. Listen to the vowel sound.

26

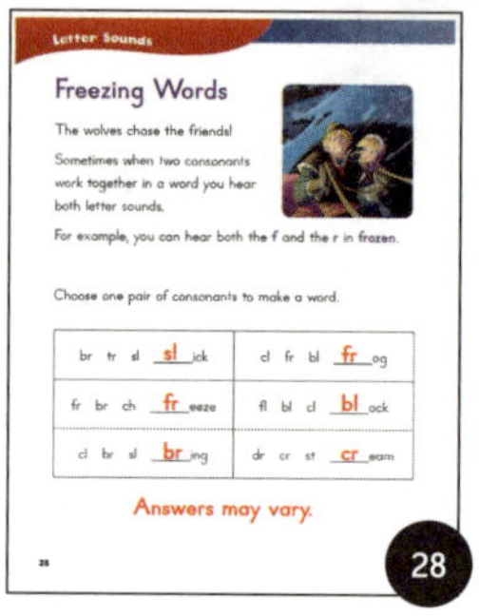

Letter Sounds

Freezing Words

The wolves chase the friends!

Sometimes when two consonants work together in a word you hear both letter sounds.

For example, you can hear both the f and the r in frozen.

Choose one pair of consonants to make a word.

br tr sl — sl ick	cl fr bl — fr og
fr br ch — fr eeze	fl bl cl — bl ock
cl br sl — br ing	dr cr st — cr eam

Answers may vary.

28

Sven pulls a sled. What two consonants work together in sled? sl

Choose one pair of consonants to make a word.

fr tr cl bl sp sl

tr ee
cl ock
fr iend
bl ow
sl ide
sp in

29

Letter Sounds

Sticking Together to the End

Two or more consonants can also work together at the end of a word.

Olaf is Anna's friend.

Listen to the sounds the letters nd make.

Choose one pair of consonants to make a word.

lp nt lt — he lp	st pt ct — te st
nt nd mp — ba nd	pt nt mp — la mp
st lp rd — bi rd	lt nt rd — elepha nt

30

Choose one pair of consonants to make a word. More than one pair of consonants may work.

st ck rd st mp nd

sti ck
be nd
du ck
grou nd
wo rd
la mp
be st

Answers may vary.

31

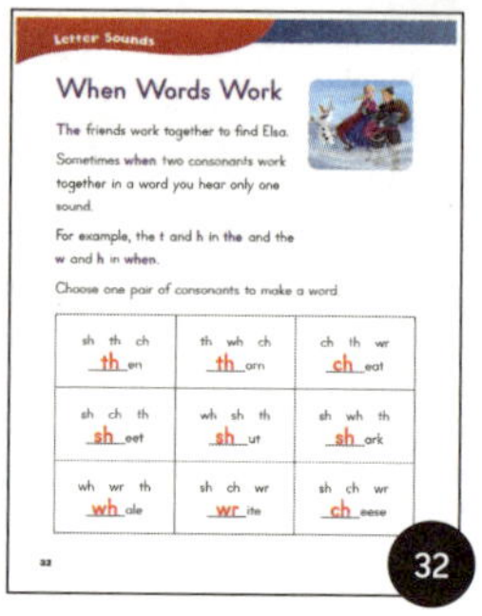

Letter Sounds

When Words Work

The friends work together to find Elsa.

Sometimes when two consonants work together in a word you hear only one sound.

For example, the t and h in the and the w and h in when.

Choose one pair of consonants to make a word.

sh th ch — th en	th wh ch — th orn	ch th wr — ch eat
sh ch th — sh eet	wh sh th — sh ut	sh wh th — sh ark
wh wr th — wh ale	sh ch wr — wr ite	sh ch wr — ch eese

32

Letter Sounds

Unfreeze the Silent Letters

Kristoff rushes to help Anna.
Elsa does not want to talk.

Did you know that letters can be silent, too?
These letters are called **silent consonants**.
The letters b, g, h, k, l, t, and w are sometimes silent.
Do you know any words with silent letters?

Say each of these words out loud.
Underline the silent letters.

castle listen lamb
two comb ghost talk hour
honest light knife sign

34

I can identify silent letters!

Say each of these words out loud.
Underline the silent letters.

walk sight wheel knee sword
when rhyme climb write knight
gnome fight wrap know

Learn Together

35

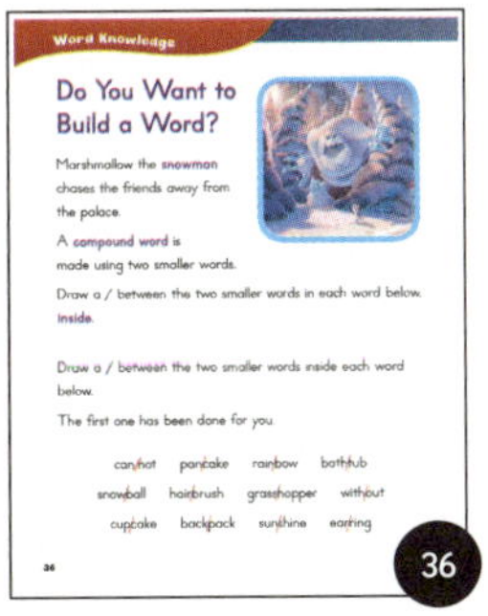
Word Knowledge

Do You Want to Build a Word?

Marshmallow the snowman chases the friends away from the palace.

A **compound word** is made using two smaller words.

Draw a / between the two smaller words in each word below.
inside

Draw a / between the two smaller words inside each word below.
The first one has been done for you.

car/hat pan/cake rain/bow bath/tub
snow/ball hair/brush grass/hopper with/out
cup/cake back/pack sun/shine ear/ring

36

I can read compound words!

Match a word on the left to a word on the right to make a compound word.

hall — way
fire — place
snow — flake
bed — room
break — fast

Circle the compound words below.

handbag glasses birthday jackpot
daydream flattery winter snowflake

Learn Together

37

Word Knowledge

Don't Look Down!

A **contraction** is a word that is made by joining two words.
An **apostrophe** takes the place of any missing letters.

Match each contraction below with the two words that have been joined.

we're — we are
don't — do not
you're — you are
he's — he is
I'm — I am

38

I can read contractions!

Fill in the missing contraction to complete each sentence.

He's don't They're

The friends run away from Marshmallow.
H e ' s upset
T h e y ' r e scared of Marshmallow.

The friends run until they reach a cliff.
They d o n ' t want to jump.

Use one of the contractions to write a sentence about Marshmallow.
Answers may vary.

Learn Together

39

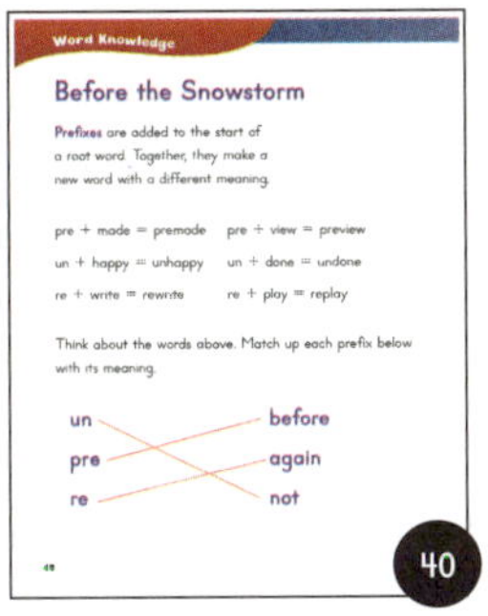
Word Knowledge

Before the Snowstorm

Prefixes are added to the start of a root word. Together, they make a new word with a different meaning.

pre + made = premade pre + view = preview
un + happy = unhappy un + done = undone
re + write = rewrite re + play = replay

Think about the words above. Match up each prefix below with its meaning.

un — not
pre — before
re — again

40

I can use prefixes to make words!

Fill in the missing prefix to complete each sentence below.

You may use each prefix more than once.

un re

Elsa is u n happy because she can't u n freeze Arendelle.
She r e plays the party in her head.
U n fortunately, Elsa will soon have more problems.
Will Elsa be able to u n do what she has done?

Add a prefix to a word to make a new word.
Answers may vary.
un + freeze = unfreeze

Learn Together

41

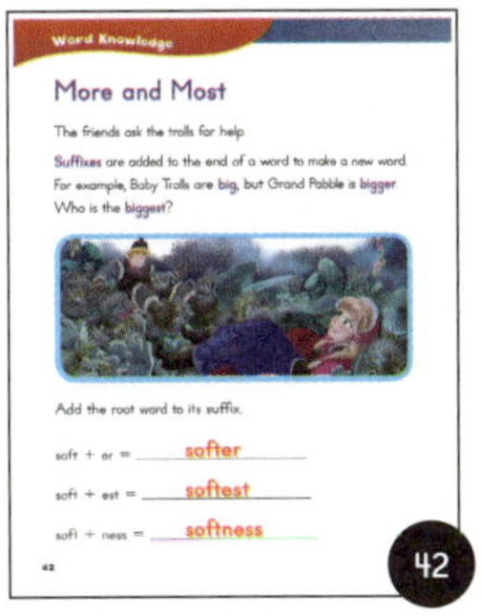
Word Knowledge

More and Most

The friends ask the trolls for help.
Suffixes are added to the end of a word to make a new word.
For example, Baby Trolls are big, but Grand Pabbie is bigger.
Who is the biggest?

Add the root word to its suffix.

soft + er = softer
soft + est = softest
soft + ness = softness

42

I can use suffixes to make words!

Try adding -er, -est, and -ness to each of the following words.

sweet sweeter sweetest sweetness
kind kinder kindest kindness
bright brighter brightest brightness

Learn Together

43

Answers

Underline the nouns in each sentence.

Anna finds Hans in the library.

"If only someone loved you Anna," Hans says with a sneer. Hans has been lying to Anna!

45

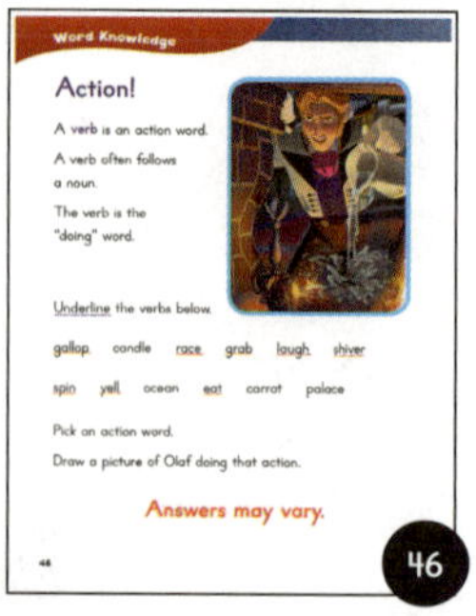
Word Knowledge

Action!

A verb is an action word.

A verb often follows a noun.

The verb is the "doing" word.

Underline the verbs below.

gallop candle race grab laugh shiver

spin yell ocean eat carrot palace

Pick an action word.

Draw a picture of Olaf doing that action.

Answers may vary.

46

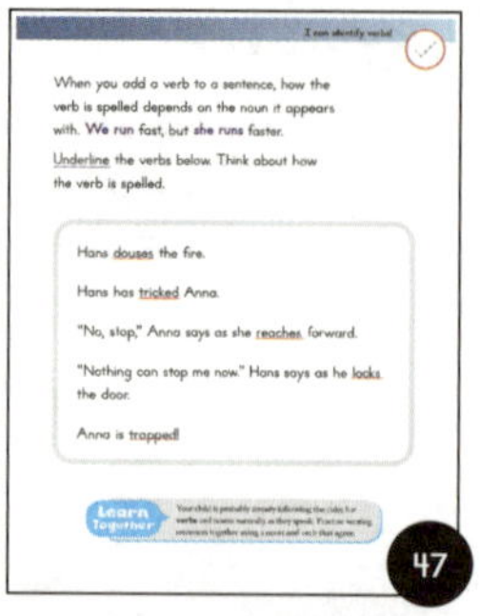
When you add a verb to a sentence, how the verb is spelled depends on the noun it appears with. We run fast, but she runs faster.

Underline the verbs below. Think about how the verb is spelled.

Hans douses the fire.

Hans has tricked Anna.

"No, stop," Anna says as she reaches forward.

"Nothing can stop me now." Hans says as he locks the door.

Anna is trapped!

47

Comprehension

Storm Over Arendelle

Clues in the text and picture can help you make predictions.

Look at the picture. Predict what the story on page 49 is about. Answers may vary.

48

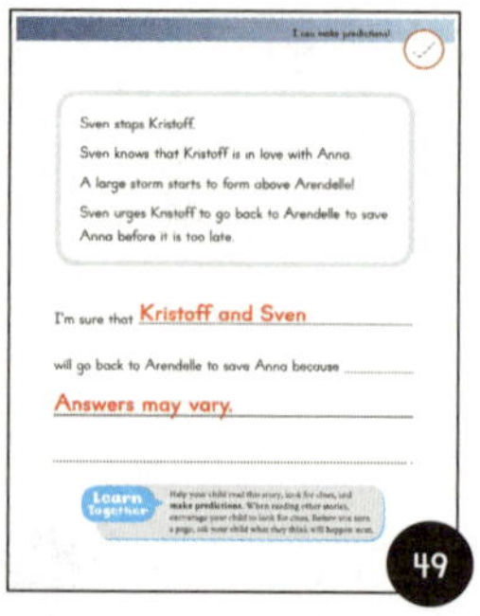
Sven stops Kristoff.

Sven knows that Kristoff is in love with Anna.

A large storm starts to form above Arendelle!

Sven urges Kristoff to go back to Arendelle to save Anna before it is too late.

I'm sure that Kristoff and Sven will go back to Arendelle to save Anna because Answers may vary.

49

Olaf looks out the window and sees Kristoff and Sven heading towards the castle.

Olaf and Anna both realize that Kristoff is the one true love that can save her.

"I have to get to Kristoff," Anna says to Olaf.

Underline the words in the story that remind you of something.

Explain any connections you made.

Answers may vary.

51

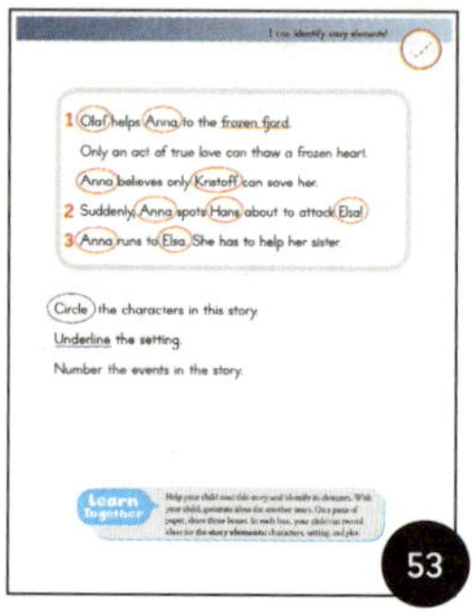
1 Olaf helps Anna to the frozen fjord.

Only an act of true love can thaw a frozen heart.

Anna believes only Kristoff can save her.

2 Suddenly, Anna spots Hans about to attack Elsa!

3 Anna runs to Elsa. She has to help her sister.

Circle the characters in this story.

Underline the setting.

Number the events in the story.

53

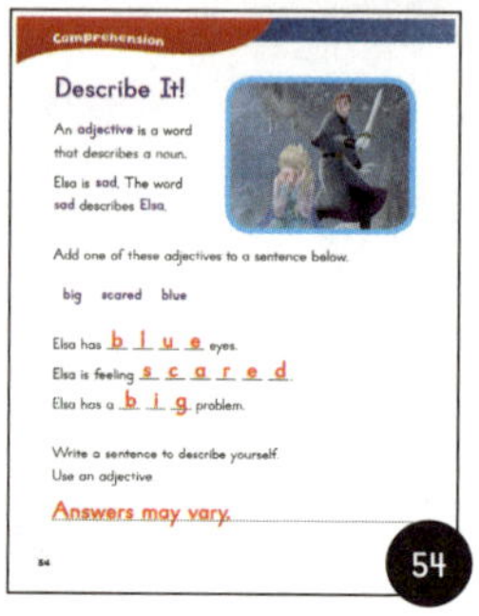
Comprehension

Describe It!

An adjective is a word that describes a noun.

Elsa is sad. The word sad describes Elsa.

Add one of these adjectives to a sentence below.

big scared blue

Elsa has b l u e eyes.

Elsa is feeling s c a r e d

Elsa has a b i g problem.

Write a sentence to describe yourself. Use an adjective.

Answers may vary.

54

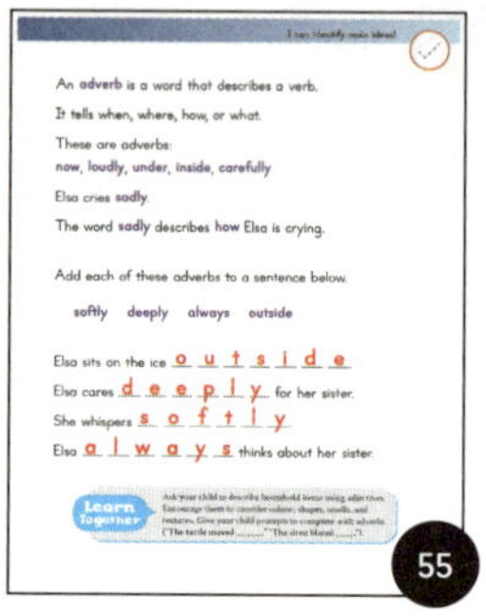
An adverb is a word that describes a verb.

It tells when, where, how, or what.

These are adverbs:

now, loudly, under, inside, carefully

Elsa cries sadly.

The word sadly describes how Elsa is crying.

Add each of these adverbs to a sentence below.

softly deeply always outside

Elsa sits on the ice o u t s i d e

Elsa cares d e e p l y for her sister.

She whispers s o f t l y

Elsa a l w a y s thinks about her sister.

55

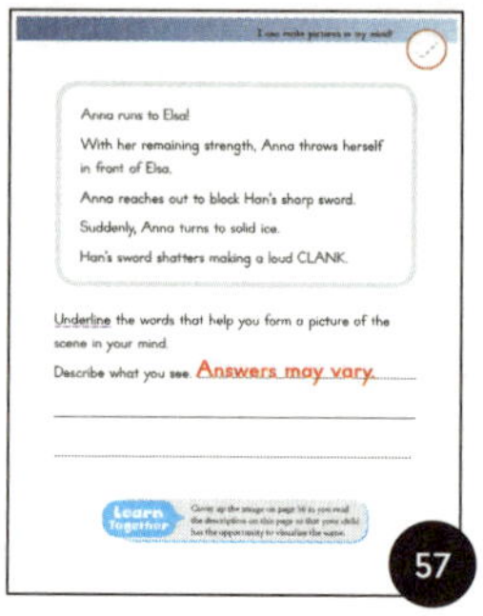
Anna runs to Elsa!

With her remaining strength, Anna throws herself in front of Elsa.

Anna reaches out to block Han's sharp sword.

Suddenly, Anna turns to solid ice.

Han's sword shatters making a loud CLANK.

Underline the words that help you form a picture of the scene in your mind.

Describe what you see. Answers may vary.

57

59

Elsa wraps her arms around her frozen sister.
Elsa begins to cry. Then something amazing happens. Suddenly, Anna begins to thaw!
"You sacrificed yourself for me?" Elsa asks.
"Of course, I love you," Anna replies.
An act of true love thaws Anna's heart.
Elsa smiles at her sister.
Elsa is happy that Anna is safe.

How do you think Elsa is feeling?

Answers may vary.

61

Hans is surprised to see that Anna is alive.
"But Elsa froze your heart," Hans says.
"The only frozen heart around here is yours," Anna declares.
Before Hans can respond Anna sends him flying with just one punch!
"That's what you get for trying to hurt my sister!" Anna states.

Do you agree with Anna's actions? Why?

Answers may vary.

63

This is a fact: Most snowmen have two eyes.
This is an opinion: I think all snowmen should be tall.
Write F beside each fact and O beside each opinion.

O I think Olaf is the best snowman.
F Snowmen are made from snow.
O Winter is better than summer.
F Ice is cold.
O I don't like sledding.
F Elsa and Anna are sisters.

64

Writing

Extra Information

Labels give you extra information.
They help you understand pictures better.
Fill in the missing labels. The first label is done for you.

hot sun
umbrella
drink
carrot
snow/Olaf

65

Captions are sentences that tell you what is happening in a picture.
They can give you more information about the picture.
Write a caption for each picture.

Answers may vary.

67

Think about a story you want to tell.
Write your story.

Answers may vary.

69

Write three facts about Anna, Elsa, or Kristoff.

1. Answers may vary.
2. Answers may vary.
3. Answers may vary.

70

Writing

Writing Sentences

Sentences end in different types of punctuation.

Kristoff is taking Anna to meet the trolls.
What is following Kristoff and Anna?

A sentence that ends with a period is telling you something.
A sentence that ends with a question mark is asking a question.

Write a sentence about Anna and Elsa that ends with a period or question mark. Answers may vary.

71

Elsa is running away!
Elsa, wait please!

A sentence that ends with an exclamation mark can show excitement or surprise.
An exclamation mark at the end of a sentence can also be a command.

Write a sentence about Anna and Elsa that ends with an exclamation mark. Answers may vary.

73

Add the missing commas to the sentences below.

I like to eat cereal oranges and oatmeal.
I like to eat cereal, orange, and oatmeal.

After breakfast I get ready for school.
After breakfast, I get ready for school.

If it is cold you should wear a hat.
If it is cold, you should wear a hat.

I like skiing skating and sledding.
I like skiing, skating, and sledding.

75

A contraction is two words put together.
The missing letters are replaced by an apostrophe.
For example, is not becomes isn't.
Make contractions with the words below, adding an apostrophe.

they have	they've	he is	he's
you are	you're	should not	shouldn't
she is	she's	let us	let's
would not	wouldn't	we are	we're
should not	shouldn't	I have	I've

76

Writing

Say It

Quotation marks show that someone is speaking. These are quotation marks: " "
These marks are often used with the words said or asked.

"This guy is a crook!" says Kristoff.
"Are you ready to go up the mountain?" Anna asks Kristoff.

Look at the picture on the right. Write what Kristoff's reply might be. Use quotation marks.

Answers may vary.

77

Write a story about a time you met someone new.
What did you say to each other?
Use quotation marks.

Answers may vary.

78

Number Sense

Speed Counts

How fast can Olaf go?
Count forward using these number lines.
Print the missing numbers.

10 20 30 40 50 60 70 80

65 70 75 80 85 90 95 100

186 188 190 192 194 196 198 200

25 50 75 100 125 150 175 200

79

Print the missing numbers on the 100-chart.

100	101	102	103	104	105	106	107	108	109
110	111	112	113	114	115	116	117	118	119
120	121	122	123	124	125	126	127	128	129
130	131	132	133	134	135	136	137	138	139
140	141	142	143	144	145	146	147	148	149
150	151	152	153	154	155	156	157	158	159
160	161	162	163	164	165	166	167	168	169
170	171	172	173	174	175	176	177	178	179
180	181	182	183	184	185	186	187	188	189
190	191	192	193	194	195	196	197	198	199	200

Answers

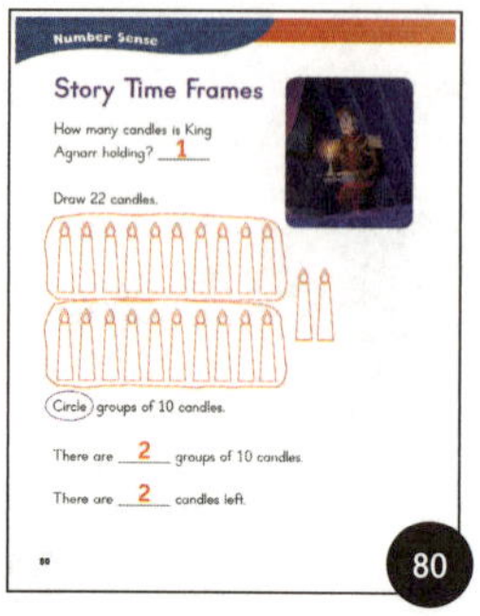
Number Sense
Story Time Frames
How many candles is King Agnarr holding? 1
Draw 22 candles.
Circle groups of 10 candles.
There are 2 groups of 10 candles.
There are 2 candles left.

80

I can represent numbers!
Show your candles in these 10-frames.
Show 22 another way.
Answers may vary.

81

Number Sense
The Greatest
Anna and Elsa are listening to great stories about the Enchanted Forest.
In each box, which number is greater?
Circle the greater number.
29 26 | 18 11 | 24 30 | 21 19
20 16 | 28 15 | 41 46 | 16 12
44 47 | 32 25 | 23 14 | 40 38

82

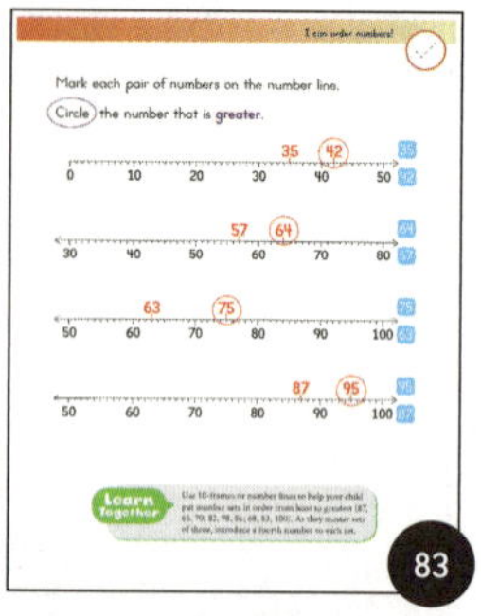
I can order numbers!
Mark each pair of numbers on the number line.
Circle the number that is greater.
35 42
57 64
63 75
87 95

83

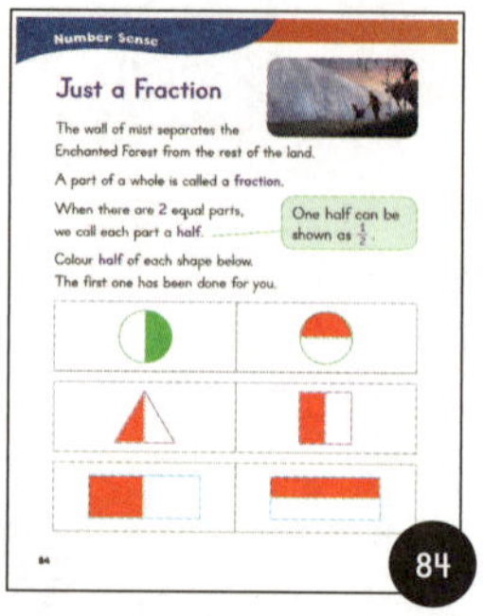
Number Sense
Just a Fraction
The wall of mist separates the Enchanted Forest from the rest of the land.
A part of a whole is called a fraction.
When there are 2 equal parts, we call each part a half.
One half can be shown as ½.
Colour half of each shape below.
The first one has been done for you.

84

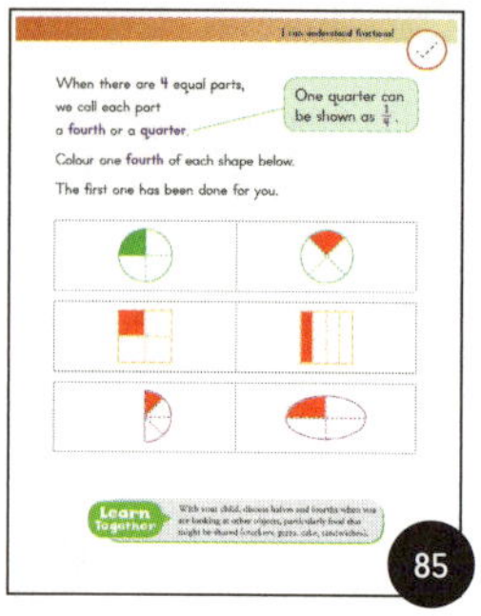
I can understand fractions!
When there are 4 equal parts, we call each part a fourth or a quarter.
One quarter can be shown as ¼.
Colour one fourth of each shape below.
The first one has been done for you.

85

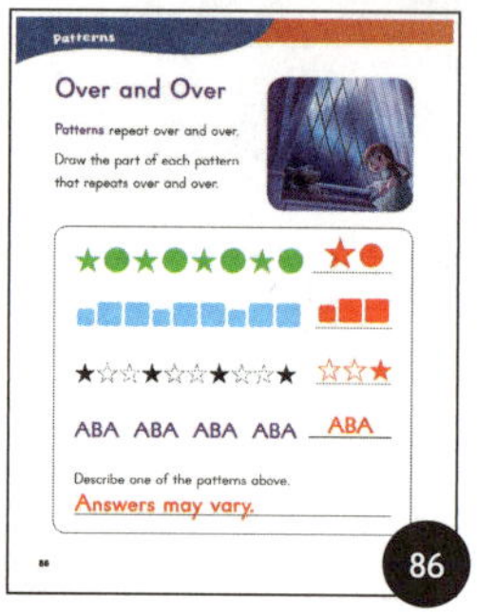
Patterns
Over and Over
Patterns repeat over and over.
Draw the part of each pattern that repeats over and over.
ABA ABA ABA ABA ABA
Describe one of the patterns above.
Answers may vary.

86

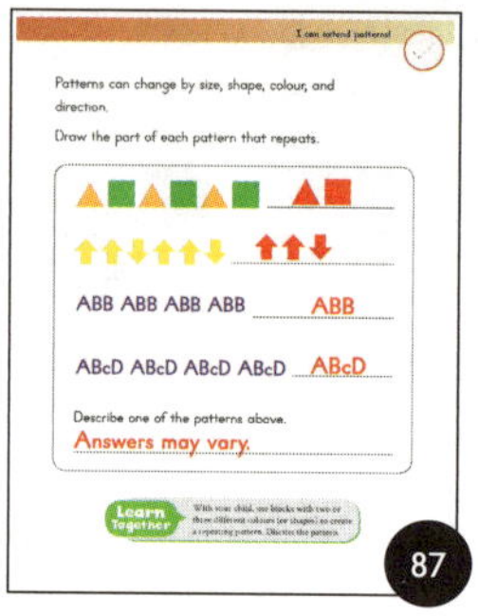
I can extend patterns!
Patterns can change by size, shape, colour, and direction.
Draw the part of each pattern that repeats.
ABB ABB ABB ABB ABB
ABcD ABcD ABcD ABcD ABcD
Describe one of the patterns above.
Answers may vary.

87

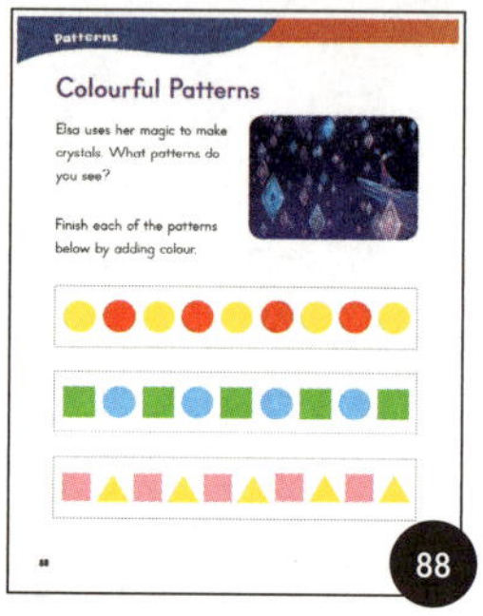
Patterns
Colourful Patterns
Elsa uses her magic to make crystals. What patterns do you see?
Finish each of the patterns below by adding colour.

88

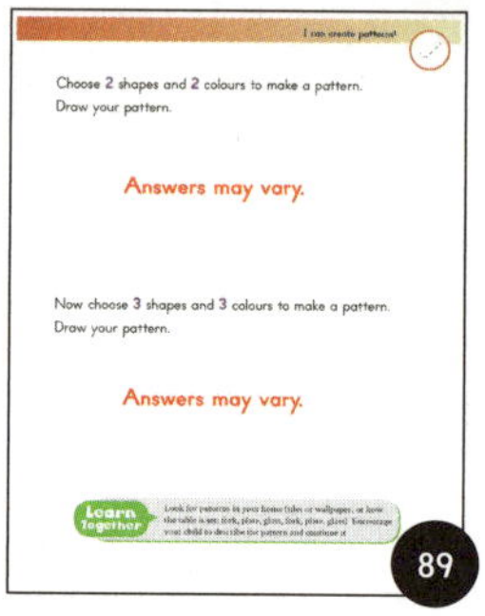
I can create patterns!
Choose 2 shapes and 2 colours to make a pattern.
Draw your pattern.
Answers may vary.
Now choose 3 shapes and 3 colours to make a pattern.
Draw your pattern.
Answers may vary.

89

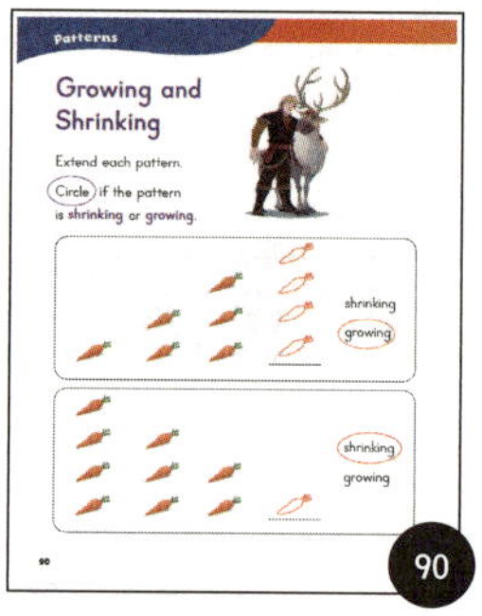
Patterns
Growing and Shrinking
Extend each pattern.
Circle if the pattern is shrinking or growing.
shrinking growing
shrinking growing

90

I can identify patterns!
Extend each pattern.
Circle if the pattern is shrinking or growing.
5 10 15 20 25 30 35 — growing
FFFFF FFFF FFF FF — shrinking
32 30 28 26 24 22 20 — shrinking

91

Addition and Subtraction
It All Adds Up
How many books does Olaf read?
3 + 6 = 9 | 9 + 9 = 18
4 + 2 = 6 | 11 + 5 = 16
7 + 10 = 17 | 4 + 8 = 12
8 + 3 = 11 | 14 + 2 = 16

92

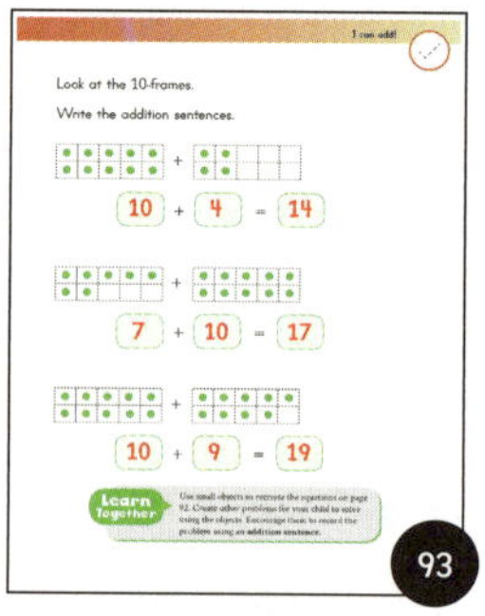
I can add!
Look at the 10-frames.
Write the addition sentences.
10 + 4 = 14
7 + 10 = 17
10 + 9 = 19

93

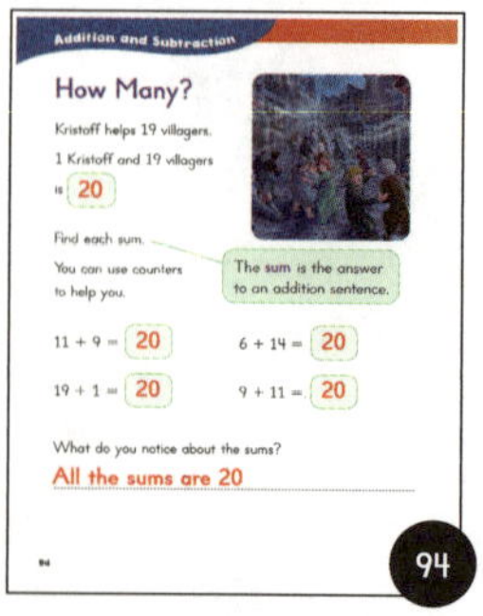
Addition and Subtraction
How Many?
Kristoff helps 19 villagers.
1 Kristoff and 19 villagers is 20
Find each sum.
You can use counters to help you.
The sum is the answer to an addition sentence.
11 + 9 = 20 | 6 + 14 = 20
19 + 1 = 20 | 9 + 11 = 20
What do you notice about the sums?
All the sums are 20

94

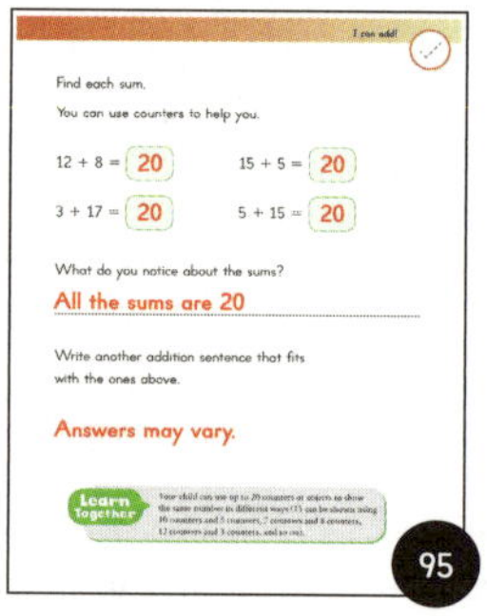
I can add!
Find each sum.
You can use counters to help you.
12 + 8 = 20 | 15 + 5 = 20
3 + 17 = 20 | 5 + 15 = 20
What do you notice about the sums?
All the sums are 20
Write another addition sentence that fits with the ones above.
Answers may vary.

95

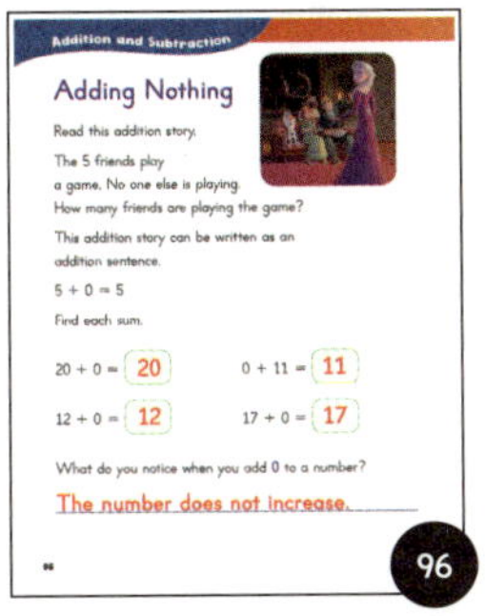
Addition and Subtraction
Adding Nothing
Read this addition story.
The 5 friends play a game. No one else is playing.
How many friends are playing the game?
This addition story can be written as an addition sentence.
5 + 0 = 5
Find each sum.
20 + 0 = 20
0 + 11 = 11
12 + 0 = 12
17 + 0 = 17
What do you notice when you add 0 to a number?
The number does not increase.
96

I can add
How many people are in this picture?
No one joins them.
Write the addition sentence for this story.
2 + 0 = 2
Find each sum.
18 + 0 = 18
0 + 25 = 25
31 + 0 = 31
0 + 14 = 14
49 + 0 = 49
50 + 0 = 50
Learn Together
97

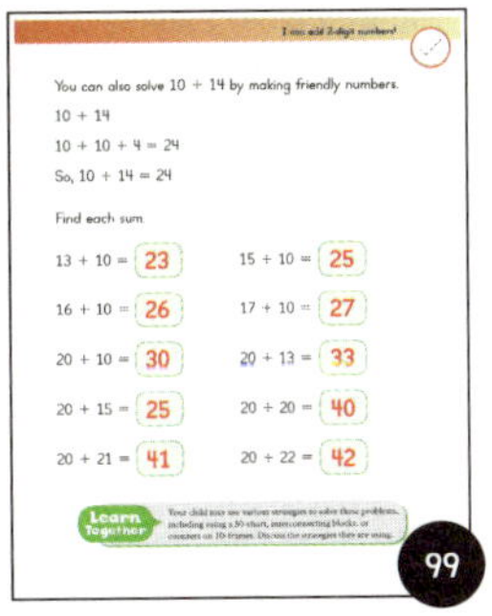
I can add 2-digit numbers!
You can also solve 10 + 14 by making friendly numbers.
10 + 14
10 + 10 + 4 = 24
So, 10 + 14 = 24
Find each sum.
13 + 10 = 23
15 + 10 = 25
16 + 10 = 26
17 + 10 = 27
20 + 10 = 30
20 + 13 = 33
20 + 15 = 25
20 + 20 = 40
20 + 21 = 41
20 + 22 = 42
Learn Together
99

Addition and Subtraction
Counting Yummy Carrots
Sven is very hungry!
There are 12 carrots.
Sven eats some carrots.
How many carrots are left?
Write the subtraction sentence.
12 − 6 = 6
12 − 4 = 8
100

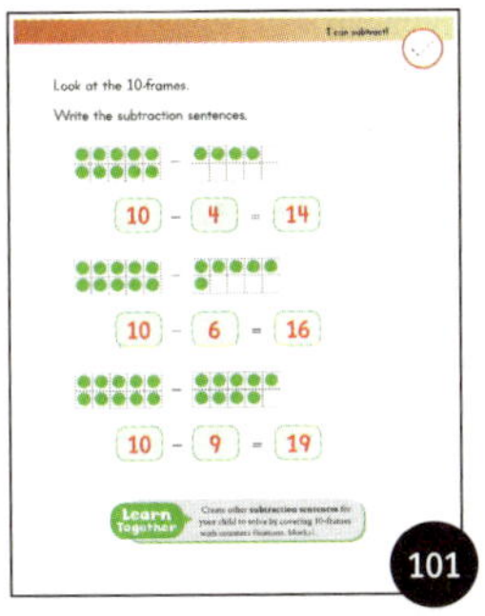
I can subtract!
Look at the 10-frames.
Write the subtraction sentences.
10 − 4 = 14
10 − 6 = 16
10 − 9 = 19
Learn Together
101

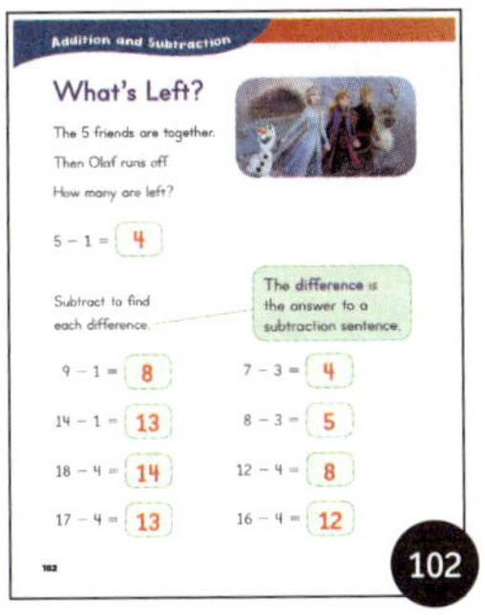
Addition and Subtraction
What's Left?
The 5 friends are together.
Then Olaf runs off.
How many are left?
5 − 1 = 4
Subtract to find each difference.
The difference is the answer to a subtraction sentence.
9 − 1 = 8
7 − 3 = 4
14 − 1 = 13
8 − 3 = 5
18 − 4 = 14
12 − 4 = 8
17 − 4 = 13
16 − 4 = 12
102

I can subtract
Anna, Elsa, and Kristoff walk together.
Anna and Kristoff lose Elsa.
How many friends are left?
3 − 1 = 2
Subtract to find each difference.
18 − 2 = 16
20 − 2 = 18
18 − 3 = 15
20 − 3 = 17
18 − 4 = 14
24 − 4 = 20
18 − 5 = 13
25 − 5 = 20
Learn Together
103

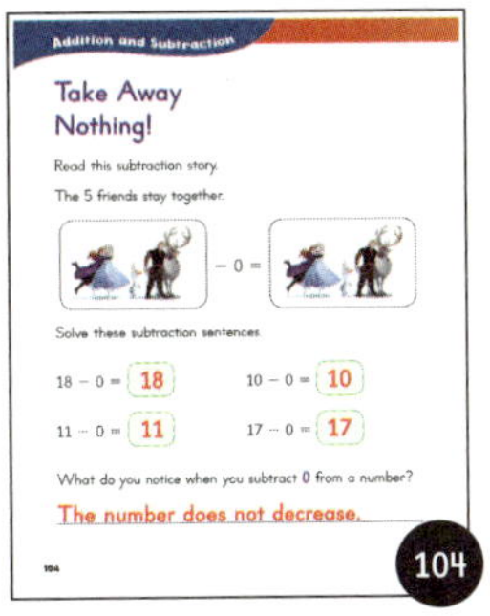
Addition and Subtraction
Take Away Nothing!
Read this subtraction story.
The 5 friends stay together.
− 0 =
Solve these subtraction sentences.
18 − 0 = 18
10 − 0 = 10
11 − 0 = 11
17 − 0 = 17
What do you notice when you subtract 0 from a number?
The number does not decrease.
104

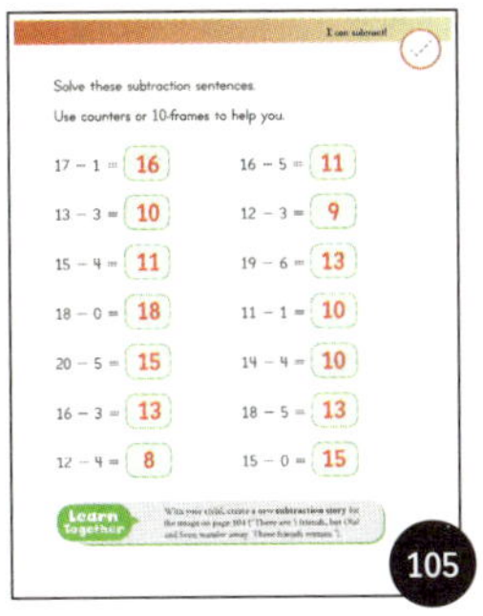
I can subtract
Solve these subtraction sentences.
Use counters or 10-frames to help you.
17 − 1 = 16
16 − 5 = 11
13 − 3 = 10
12 − 3 = 9
15 − 4 = 11
19 − 6 = 13
18 − 0 = 18
11 − 1 = 10
20 − 5 = 15
14 − 4 = 10
16 − 3 = 13
18 − 5 = 13
12 − 4 = 8
15 − 0 = 15
Learn Together
105

Addition and Subtraction
Cloudy Calculations
The monoliths are covered in misty clouds.
What can you add or subtract to change the first number into the final number?
The first one is done for you.
20 − 2 = 18
7 + 11 = 18
8 + 11 = 19
17 − 6 = 11
12 + 11 = 3
20 + 5 = 25
5 + 10 = 15
16 − 12 = 4
106

I can relate addition and subtraction!
7 + 2 = 5
24 − 12 = 12
11 + 4 = 15
13 + 8 = 21
9 + 8 = 17
22 + 3 = 25
16 − 4 = 12
15 − 6 = 9
25 − 5 = 20
14 + 7 = 21
8 − 4 = 4
8 + 6 = 14
20 − 10 = 10
10 + 10 = 20
Learn Together
107

Multiplication and Division
Joining Equal Groups
You multiply when you join equal groups.
Here are 4 groups of 2 crystals.
There are 8 crystals altogether.
4 × 2 = 8
This is another way to show the word multiply.
Here are 2 groups of 3 crystals.
There are 6 crystals altogether.
108

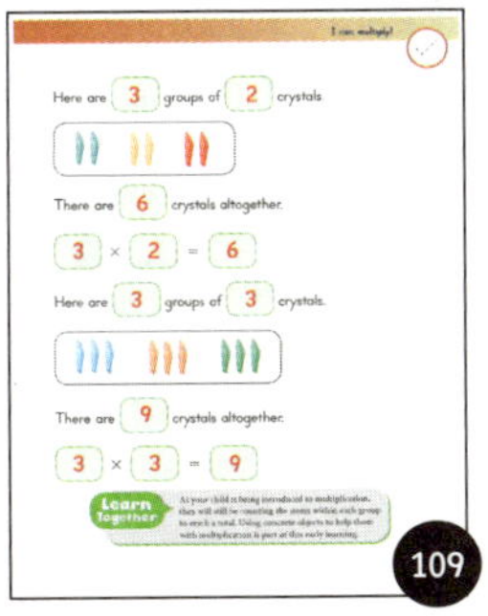
I can multiply!
Here are 3 groups of 2 crystals.
There are 6 crystals altogether.
3 × 2 = 6
Here are 3 groups of 3 crystals.
There are 9 crystals altogether.
3 × 3 = 9
Learn Together
109

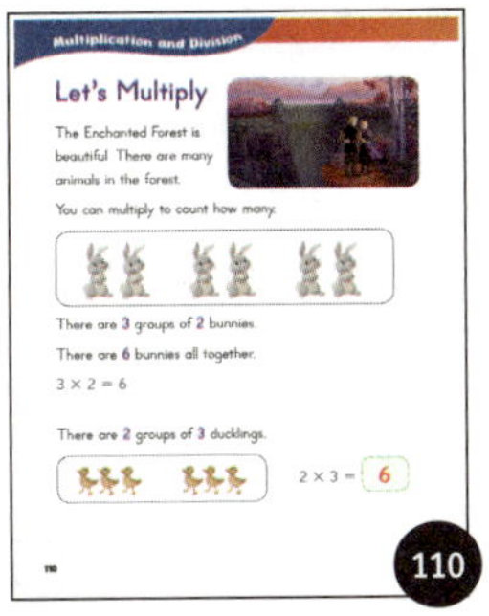
Multiplication and Division
Let's Multiply
The Enchanted Forest is beautiful. There are many animals in the forest.
You can multiply to count how many.
There are 3 groups of 2 bunnies.
There are 6 bunnies all together.
3 × 2 = 6
There are 2 groups of 3 ducklings.
2 × 3 = 6
110

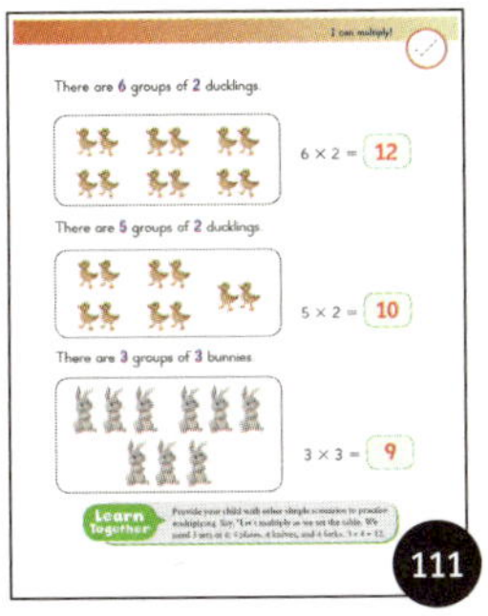
I can multiply!
There are 6 groups of 2 ducklings.
6 × 2 = 12
There are 5 groups of 2 ducklings.
5 × 2 = 10
There are 3 groups of 3 bunnies.
3 × 3 = 9
Learn Together
111

Multiplication and Division
Counting Groups
The Enchanted Forest is beautiful. Olaf counts the leaves on the trees.
Circle every group of 2 leaves.
Fill in the boxes.
2 + 2 + 2 + 2 + 2 = 10
There are 5 groups of 2.
5 × 2 = 10
There are 10 leaves.
112

Answers

113

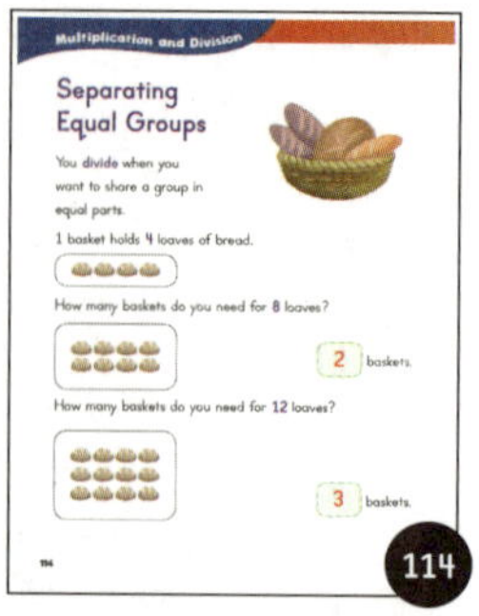
114

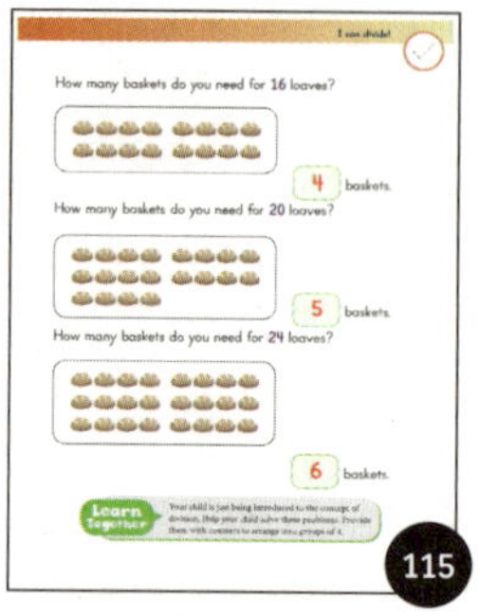
115

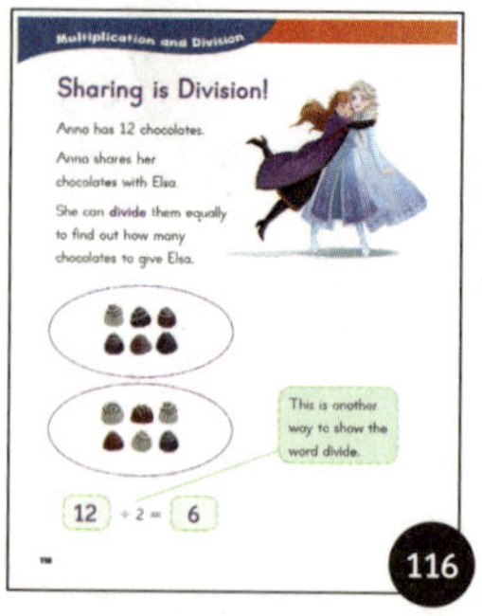
116

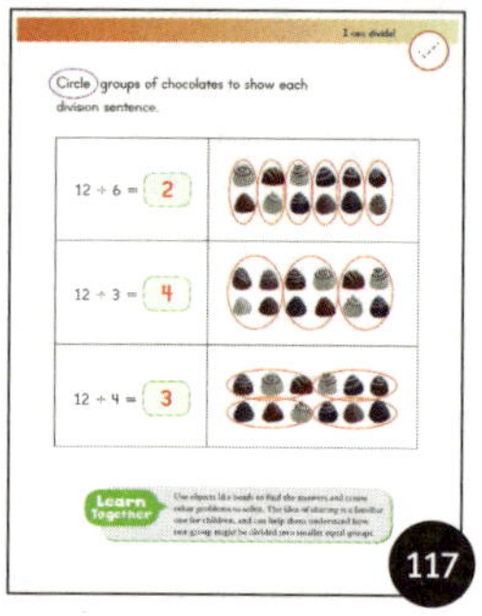
117

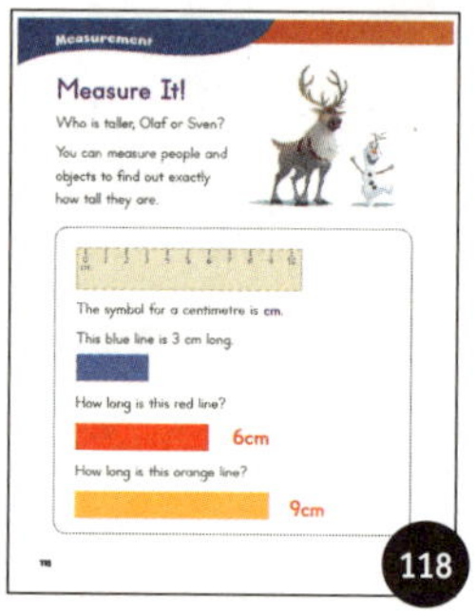
118

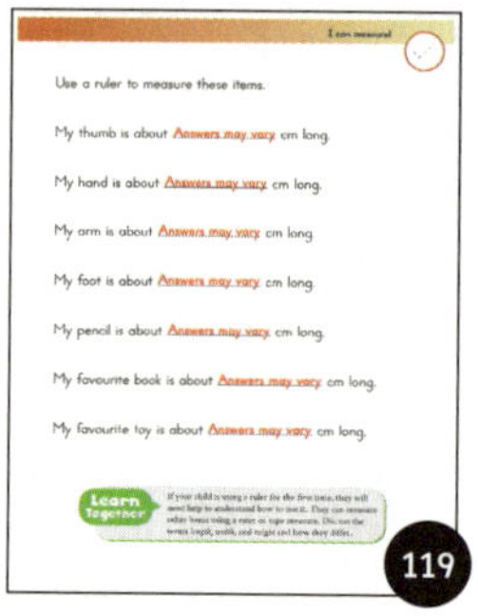
119

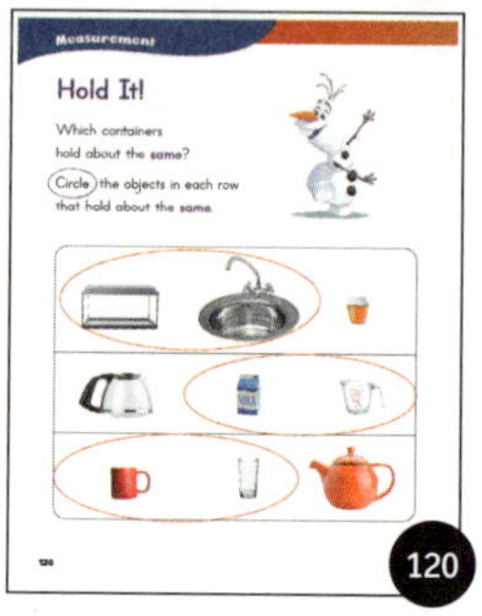
120

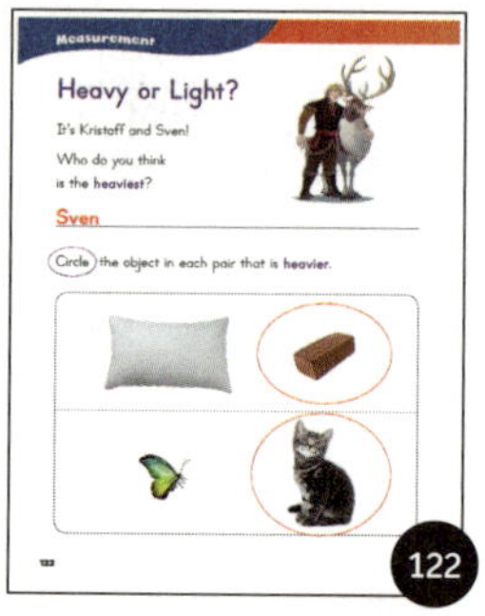
122

124

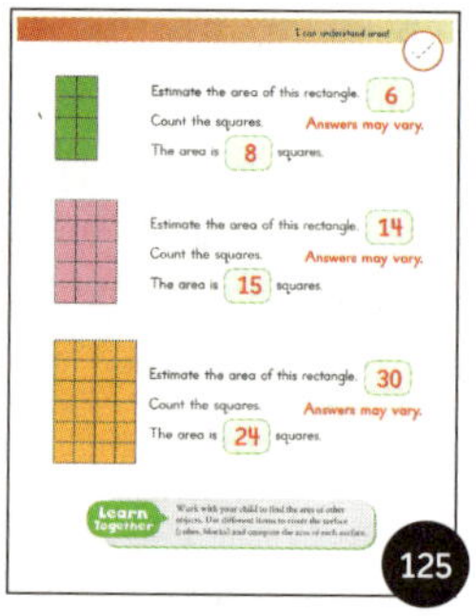
125

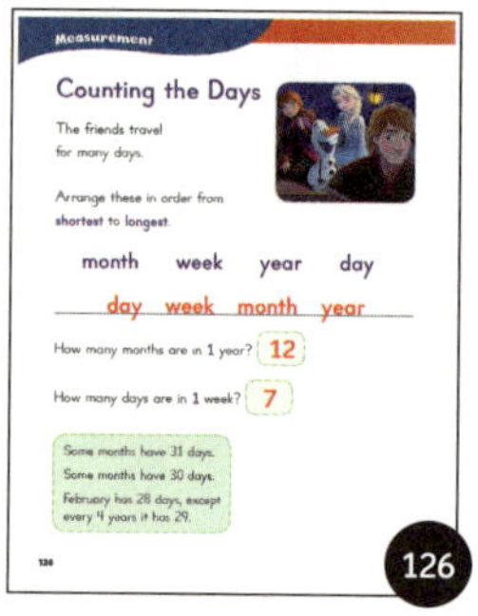
126

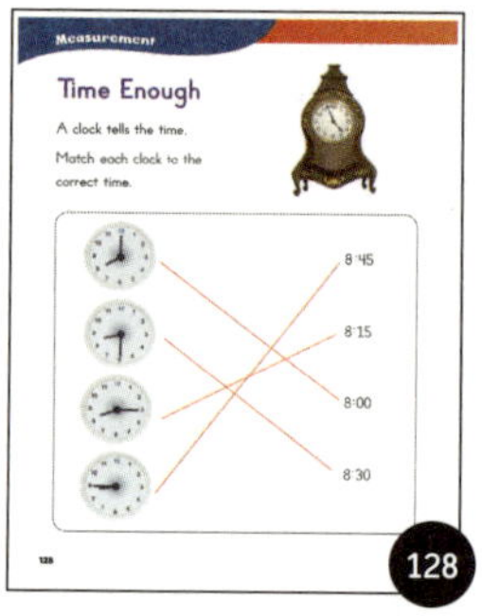
128

130

131

132

133

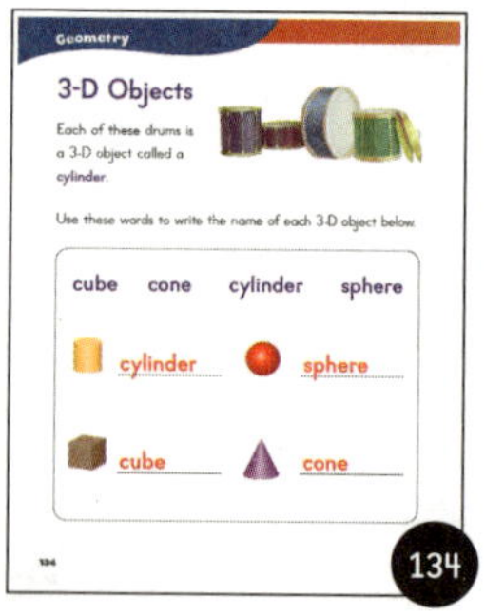
134

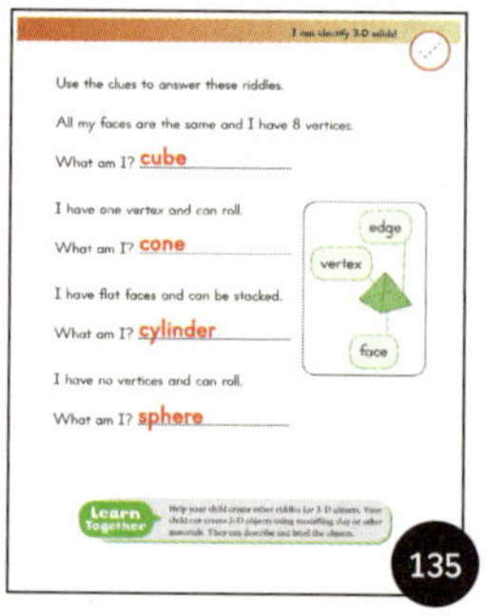
135

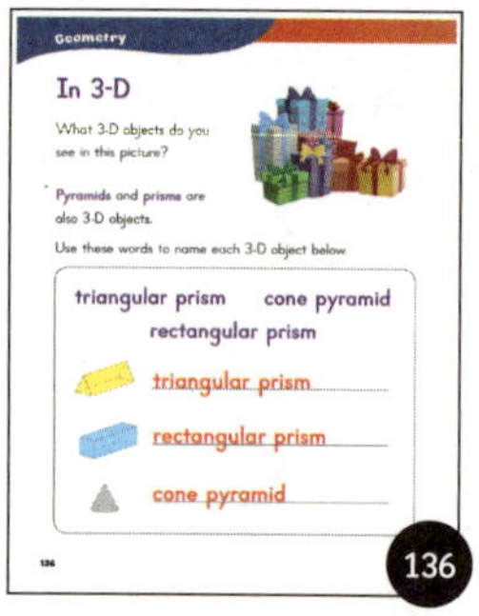
136

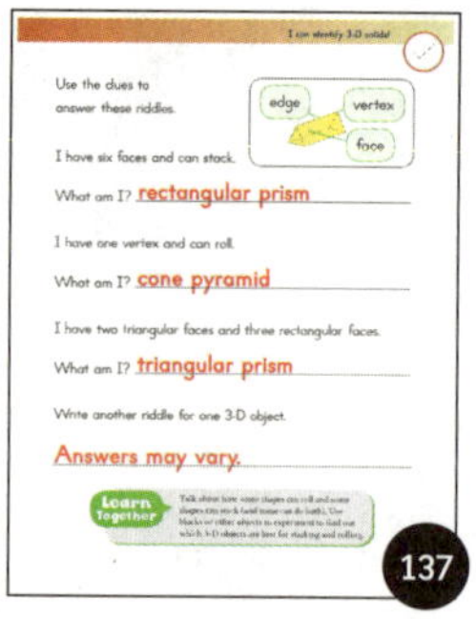
137

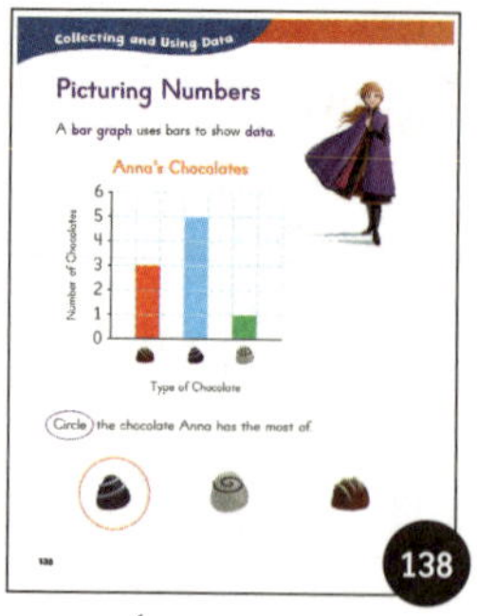
138

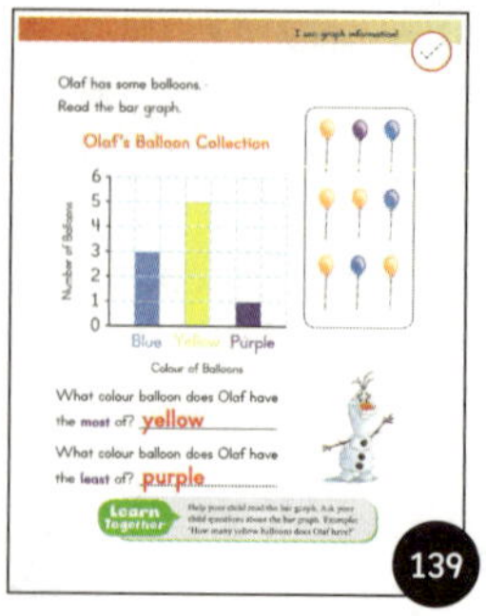
139

140